Nelly Custis

CHILD OF MOUNT VERNON

Nelly Custis

CHILD OF MOUNT VERNON

DAVID L. RIBBLETT

Introduction by
Julie Nixon Eisenhower

MOUNT VERNON LADIES' ASSOCIATION

MOUNT VERNON, VIRGINIA

1993

LIBRARY OF CONGRESS CATALOGING-IN-PUBLICATION DATA
RIBBLETT, DAVID L., 1958-
NELLY CUSTIS: CHILD OF MOUNT VERNON/BY DAVID L. RIBBLETT;
INTRODUCTION BY JULIE NIXON EISENHOWER.
P. CM.
INCLUDES BIBLIOGRAPHICAL REFERENCES AND INDEX.
ISBN 0-931917-23-9 (SOFTCOVER)
1. LEWIS, NELLY CUSTIS, 1779-1852. 2. PRESIDENTS—UNITED STATES—GRANDCHILDREN—BIOGRAPHY.
3.WASHINGTON, GEORGE, 1732-1799—FAMILY. 4. WASHINGTON FAMILY. I. TITLE.
E312. 19.L53 1993
973.5 ' 092—DC20
[B]

93-12419
CIP

FRONT COVER: "ELEANOR PARKE CUSTIS" BY ROBERT EDGE PINE, 1785.
MOUNT VERNON LADIES' ASSOCIATION.
BACK COVER: "MRS. LAWRENCE LEWIS" BY GILBERT STUART, *CIRCA* 1805.
NATIONAL GALLERY OF ART, WASHINGTON.
GIFT OF H.H. WALKER LEWIS IN MEMORY OF HIS PARENTS, MR. AND MRS. EDWIN A.S. LEWIS.

BOOK DESIGN BY
GLENN A. HENNESSEY
WASHINGTON, DC

to my mother

B . M . R .

A c k n o w l e d g m e n t s

At the age of 10, I visited Mount Vernon for the first time with my parents. I carried away with me as a souvenir a book entitled Mount Vernon Is Ours: The Story of the Preservation and Restoration of Washington's Home, *by Elswyth Thane. It inspired and launched my interest in historic homes, their occupants and their restorations. Years later, after researching and writing many articles on historic homes, I returned to Mount Vernon, this time to write a book of my own. At Mount Vernon, I have come to learn that the home of George Washington is, indeed,* ours. *As Americans it is our duty to preserve it and keep its history alive.*

It is a pleasure to thank the people who came to my aid during the research and writing of this manuscript. The Mount Vernon Ladies' Association and its staff: James C. Rees, associate director; Neil W. Horstman, resident director; the publications committee; Ellen McCallister Clark, former librarian who first suggested Nelly to me; John P. Riley, historian; Barbara A. McMillan, librarian; Christine Meadows, curator; Mary V. Thompson, curatorial registrar; Anne Huber Gorham, assistant curator and former curator of Woodlawn; and to Jean S. Corley, Shirley C. Krein, Virginia A. Prince and Carter King Laughlin. And especially warm thanks go to Ann M. Rauscher, manager of media relations, who was involved with this project from the early planning stage, through the research and writing, and finally to publication.

I also wish to express my appreciation to three people, who by their knowledge, encouragement and generosity have been a tremendous inspiration to me and my writing: Larry J. Cameron, E. Joyce Schanze and Rebecca V. Jackson.

My parents have always made clear their belief in me, and I appreciate their love and support.

David L. Ribblett
Richmond, Virginia

INTRODUCTION

In reading this new and fascinating biography of Nelly Custis, I found myself reflecting upon how circumstances have changed in the 200 years since her "grandpapa" was elected our first president. Although President Washington faced tremendous challenges and was constantly setting the standards for the future, one might describe his family life as exciting but normal. The Washingtons lived without a Secret Service agent behind every corner, with few reporters to avoid, and not a single camera to interrupt the privacy so treasured by both George and Martha Washington. Recalling my own days in the White House, I am truly envious of this bygone era.

Yet I realize that Nelly Custis did indeed experience the same trials and tribulations of most presidential children and grandchildren who come of age in the White House. There is no question that her years in the presidential household dramatically changed Nelly's life — just as they did mine, and just as they will continue to change the lives of the children, grandchildren, nieces and nephews of our future leaders.

My father became vice president when I was only four years old, and I was barely out of my teens and newly-married when he was inaugurated as president. My sister Tricia and I followed in the footsteps of Lynda and Luci Johnson, Margaret Truman, Alice Roosevelt and other young women who faced the unique challenges of trying to maintain a normal life under the eyes of what at times seemed to be the entire nation.

For us, Nelly Custis was a ground breaker. No one had paved the way for her; indeed, the role of the president's family has never been clearly defined, before or since. Fortunately, Nelly was an attractive, personable and strong-willed young lady when she arrived in New York with her grandmother. While Mrs. Washington began her term as First Lady with a stoic sense of duty, rather than a feeling of excitement and anticipation, Nelly seems to have relished the chance to take center stage. Surviving letters from the presidential years tell us that she captured the hearts of Washington's colleagues and made visits to the Washington home a more memorable experience. The strains of Nelly practicing on her harpsichord surely must have made a meeting with the president a slightly less ominous affair. During the darkest moments of Washington's term, he was grateful to have his bright-eyed granddaughter so close at hand.

It is exciting to witness the blossoming of Nelly Custis, to see her evolve from a girl to an intelligent and musically gifted young woman, sought after by a variety of suitors. It is equally interesting to observe her total devotion to her grandparents and the emptiness she felt when George and Martha Washington died, and their grand Mount Vernon estate lost its guiding force.

Between the lines, this book tells us a great deal about George Washington's character. All Americans relate to Washington as a masterful soldier and a president beyond reproach, but through Nelly's eyes, we see a different person. We view Washington not as the "Father of Our Country," but as the grandfather of a high-spirited teenager, a man of gentle and wise advice. My admiration for Washington — already greater than my words can adequately convey — has increased since reading Nelly's story. I must admire the solidarity in the Washingtons' presidential household, the loyalty and caring between family members that cannot be disrupted by any outside force.

Readers should be forewarned that the life of Nelly Custis is by no means a fairy tale. I have yet to learn of a child or grandchild of a president who has not experienced the difficult side of living in a presidential household. The indescribable stress of the presidency, in the 18th century as well as today, is shared by the family. As she became a mother and grandmother herself, Nelly learned that her "grandpapa" could not protect her from all of life's problems. Yet as the plantation system crumbled and her family scattered, Nelly still held on to her memories of Mount

Vernon's "golden age," and her unforgettable years as the most celebrated teenager in America.

Unfortunately, it is rare for historians to reflect upon the accomplishments and challenges faced by women in colonial and federal periods. In Nelly Custis, we discover a fresh and fascinating character lifted from a critical period of American history. And through her eyes, we gain a new perspective on George Washington, the "Father of Our Country."

JULIE NIXON EISENHOWER

PROLOGUE

When Eleanor Parke Custis Lewis died in 1852, the *Philadelphia Inquirer* reported her passing under the headline "Death of a Distinguished Lady." Born at the peak of the Revolutionary War and dying less than 10 years before the outbreak of the Civil War, her life was lived against a background of momentous historical events, particularly those associated with our country's greatest hero. Her place in history was assured by her unique relationship with George Washington, her stepgrandfather, under whose roof she was raised. Nelly went to live at Mount Vernon just before General Washington returned home from the war, and the family enjoyed a peaceful interlude there before he once again answered the call of his country. As a member of the president's household, Nelly was a firsthand observer of Washington's often tumultuous eight years as the country's first chief executive. These years were Nelly's own golden years. She then returned with the Washingtons to Mount Vernon, where the former president contentedly lived out his retirement years.

Through Nelly's eyes one sees her "Grandpapa" in a human light as a caring father and attentive guardian, rather than as an icon inscribed with the words "Father of His Country." A concerned father emerges who worries about his foster daughter's education and her courtships, and attempts to launch her happiness after her marriage. Nelly claimed she was never in awe of George Washington as others were. She made him laugh, she made him proud, and she showed him enormous devotion and respect throughout her life.

When Nelly was 10 years old, George Washington became the first president, and she and her little brother became the first presidential children. Although the new Constitution was somewhat specific about the role of president, her role as a member of the first family was not described. Nevertheless, she anxiously took advantage of the opportunities that this new position afforded her. One of the biggest changes Nelly experienced was the family's move from peaceful Mount Vernon to the thriving capital cities of New York and Philadelphia, which offered a lively young girl many more educational opportunities as well as exciting attractions and entertainments. To Martha Washington fell the job of restraining her spirited granddaughter and coaching her in the areas of dress, manners and moral values. At the president's house, Nelly occasionally entertained members of Congress on her harpsichord, and she engaged them in conversation that proved her political opinions were learned at her stepgrandfather's knee. By all accounts she rose to every occasion. And, although President Washington disliked any comparison of the American presidency to Great Britain's royalty, the beautiful Nelly Custis became an "American Princess."

Nelly's early years were unlike most other girls of her era. But the latter half of her life was more typical, and the adjustment was not an easy one for her to make. When one century changed into another, Nelly Custis represented a historical bridge between the eras. Her life changed as well. The Washingtons, her guardians and guides, were gone. She had the challenging responsibilities of a mistress of a Virginia plantation. Her husband turned out to lack the motivation and stamina that Nelly had expected in a mate and provider. And she bore eight children, seven of whom she buried with tragic regularity. In the new century, Virginia's gentry changed their attitudes toward success, love, religion, and death. Nelly's experiences echoed these changes. The remainder of Nelly Custis's life was lived out like every American's, trying to do the best for herself and her family in what proved for her to be an often elusive pursuit of happiness.

THE

MOUNT

VERNON

YEARS

CHAPTER ONE

"The Little Folks"

On September 9, 1781, General George Washington stopped at Mount Vernon for a brief respite on his way to another confrontation with the British army, this time at Yorktown, Virginia. For the first time in six years he stood on the soil of his beloved plantation. Besides his wife Martha, the welcoming party included her son Jacky Custis and his wife Eleanor, who had come from their home Abingdon along with their four children. Ranging in age from five years to five months, Washington's step-grandchildren were all born while he was away serving as commander in chief of the Continental Army. The children had already developed personalities of their own. Willful Eliza Parke Custis, serene Martha Parke Custis, fair Eleanor Parke Custis and the baby George Washington Parke Custis all knew Mount Vernon as their second home. Eleanor Parke, named for her mother but called "Nelly," had spent more time under her grandparents' roof than her siblings. Because of Nelly's mother's poor health after her daughter's birth on March 31, 1779, the child was sent to Mount Vernon to be nursed. Two years later, after the birth and death of twins, little Washington was born, and he joined his sister at Mount Vernon.

General Washington's homecoming was short-lived, lasting only three days. By then the French officers, General Rochambeau and his staff, had arrived at Mount Vernon to accompany Washington to Yorktown, where the French allies under General Lafayette had cornered General Cornwallis and his

British troops on the Virginia peninsula below Williamsburg. During their brief stay the foreign officers admired the general's newly enlarged mansion house and the surrounding plantation, proudly shown to them by their host. In the upper garden, the Frenchmen were particularly delighted by the appearance of a number of hummingbirds, which they had never seen before. Before the officers continued their ride southward, Jacky Custis announced his plans to join his stepfather's army, in spite of the fact that he was still recuperating from an illness that had stricken him earlier that fall. General Washington was pleased to enlist Jacky as a volunteer aide-de-camp on his staff. After he arrived in Yorktown, Jacky wrote a note of comfort to his mother, "I have the pleasure to inform you that I find myself much better since I left Mount Vernon."

Seven weeks after Washington left home, Cornwallis surrendered at Yorktown on October 17, 1781. The war for independence was nearing an end. Neither General Washington nor his stepson celebrated, however, because Jacky was suffering from camp fever, which had erupted during the final days of the siege. Washington had his stepson conveyed to Eltham in New Kent County, the home of Burwell Bassett, Martha's widowed brother-in-law. Jacky was attended by Dr. James Craik, Washington's life-long physician and friend. When the patient's condition worsened, his wife and mother were summoned. After four days of travel, Eleanor, Martha and five-year-old Eliza arrived at his bedside. On November 5, 1781, 22 days before his 28th birthday, Jacky Custis died, leaving his four young children without a father. He was buried in Eltham's garden.

Washington escorted his wife, Jacky's young widow and her child back to Mount Vernon, where he stayed long enough to begin settling his stepson's tangled business affairs. With Martha's permission he wrote a letter to her brother Bartholomew Dandridge, asking him to be the administrator of his nephew's estate. As the closest male relative on their father's side, Washington also asked Dandridge to take on the legal care of the fatherless children, but Dandridge refused. The general then marched with his army to the north where the British still held New York. Two years later, word came at last that the peace treaty had been signed in Paris, and the war ended on November 25, 1783, when the British finally abandoned their last stonghold. General Washington said farewell to his officers at Fraunces' Tavern in New York City, stopped and purchased gifts for the grandchildren in Philadelphia, and resigned his commission in Annapolis, the temporary seat of Congress. He turned his horse up the familiar driveway at Mount Vernon on Christmas Eve. Nelly's earliest remembrance was running to meet her Grandpapa upon his arrival home. Washington wrote to Lafayette that he had "on the eve of Christmas entered these doors, an older man by nine years, than when I left them."

With the Custis children gathered around, Grandpapa spilled from his trunks an array of presents, including a cap, a locket, a handkerchief, a whirligig, a fiddle, a quadrille box, dress sashes and pocket books. The children were enchanted. Soon after, their mother announced to the Washingtons her plans to marry Dr. David Stuart, a widower who had recently started his medical practice in nearby Alexandria. The sudden announcement should not have come as a complete surprise to Washington, since his cousin and estate manager, Lund Washington, had informed the general of that possibility during the last days of the war. But Washington had remained skeptical, writing back from his headquarters in Rocky Hill, New York, "Mrs. Custis has never suggested in any of her Letters to Mrs. Washington . . . the most distant attachment to D. S." The son of a minister, Dr. Stuart attended the College of William and Mary and had a medical degree from the University of Edinburgh. Nelly's sister, Eliza Custis, would later write, "He had just returned from Europe . . . where he received every advantage of Education and was one of the most learned men of his day." Washington respected Stuart's maturity, and he approved of his solid education and established business, assets that Jacky Custis lacked when he married Eleanor Calvert 10 years before. Washington gave the couple his blessing. "Two years after my father's departure," Eliza wrote, "my mother gave her hand to Dr. Stuart . . . . She chose the man who she believed would make the best guardian for her children." Stuart planned to take the two youngest Custis children back to live with their older sisters at Abingdon, located on the banks of the Potomac River a short distance above Alexandria.

After the wedding, however, the guardianship of the Custis children was still in doubt. In June 1784, Washington was still pressing Bartholomew Dandridge to take on the responsibility of being the children's guardian. Washington could perceive Dandridge's unwillingness to take the children, and he did not understand why their uncle could not see his duty. Washington wanted the situation cleared up because the unsettled matter added to Martha's grief at the loss of her last surviving child. By the age of 50, Martha had witnessed the deaths of all her children.

By her first husband, Daniel Parke Custis, Martha had four children, two of whom survived infancy. By the time Martha married Washington, Jacky had almost forgotten his own father, and Patsy had never really known him. In June of 1773, 14 years after their marriage, Patsy died of an epileptic seizure at the age of 17. The month before her death, Washington, who was extremely frustrated by Jacky's indifference to school and his frequent irresponsible behavior, had enrolled his stepson at New York College. After Patsy's death, Jacky's distance from his mother added to her sorrow. Washington wrote to Martha's brother, "This sudden and unexpected blow, I scarce need add, has reduced my poor wife to the lowest ebb of misery; which is increased by the absence of her son." Jacky, who was not interested in continuing his education, told his mother he would gladly return home because his presence there would ease her suffering. That was the end of Jacky's schooling.

The following February, Jacky, age 19, married 16-year-old Eleanor Calvert at Mount Airy, her family home in Maryland. Washington attended the ceremony, but Martha remained at Mount Vernon, fearing that her melancholy state since the death of Patsy would cast a gloom on the festivities. When the war for independence began, Washington was disappointed in Jacky's lack of interest in taking any active part in the war. Washington thought that if Jacky was not going to join the army, his place was with his mother. "At any time," Washington wrote after he was given command of the Continental Army, "I hope it is unnecessary for me to say that I am always pleased with your and Nellie's [Eleanor Calvert Custis] abidance at Mount Vernon; much less upon this occasion, when I think it is absolutely necessary for the peace and satisfaction of your mother; a consideration which I have no doubt will have due weight with you both, and require no arguments to enforce." During the long war, Martha visited her husband for several months each year at his winter quarters, and when she was home she often enjoyed the companionship of her son's growing family.

At the end of the war, Jacky was in his grave, and because of the remarriage of his wife, it seemed likely that Martha would be separated from her two youngest grandchildren as well. The loss would be more than Martha could bear. And so it was decided that Nelly and little Washington would remain at Mount Vernon, where they had spent most of their lives. There is evidence that in a time when the mortality rate was so high, particularly among children, losses were not irreparable. Love could be transferred from one child to another, and, in a sense, Nelly and her brother replaced the children Martha had lost. The Washingtons became the Custis children's foster parents, although they were not legally adopted as we know the term today. Still it became the duty of the Washingtons not only to love and protect the children and take on the financial responsibilities necessary for their upbringing, but also to provide them with the proper moral and educational background as well.

Historians have given the impression that Eleanor Custis Stuart was all too willing to hand her children over to the Washingtons. Although she was sympathetic with Martha's feelings of deprivation, Eleanor did not relinquish the care of her children without uncertainty, particularly her youngest daughter. She later wrote, "But what cou'd I do? It wou'd have been barbarous to have

NELLY CUSTIS IS SEEN WALKING BESIDE GEORGE AND MARTHA WASHINGTON
IN THIS 1792 PAINTING OF THE WEST FRONT OF MOUNT VERNON,
ATTRIBUTED TO EDWARD SAVAGE. THE PAINTING AND ITS COMPANION EAST
FRONT VIEW ARE THE EARLIEST KNOWN VIEWS OF THE MANSION.
MOUNT VERNON LADIES' ASSOCIATION.

taken her from her Grandmama . . . . She was quite unhappy."
Also to be considered was the effect of separating Nelly from her
sisters, Eliza and Martha. In this regard Eleanor was thinking
more of her two older daughters when she wrote, "It wou'd be a
pity there shou'd be so great a difference in their advantages."
Her concern was prophetic, but still she agreed to let her children
remain at Mount Vernon, and she wrote that she was "obliged to
submit," suggesting she was under some pressure. Her decision
would haunt her. Regarding her role as a mother to her two
youngest children, she would one day write, "For there is not an

hour in the Day that I do not accuse myself of a failure." Eleanor did not recede from the lives of Nelly and little Washington. She and her older daughters visited them often, and she was not so much intimidated by the Washingtons that she did not occasionally find fault with their methods of raising her children.

At Mount Vernon it seemed as if time had turned back 25 years. Again there were two small children playing in the mansion house and gardens, just as Jacky and Patsy had done a generation before. After his return from the war, Washington wrote that as a result of illness Nelly was "in a puny state." But one year later he was able to report, "the little folks enjoy perfect health." Mount Vernon had a healing effect on their grandfather as well. Here, "under the shadow of my own Vine and Fig-tree, free from the bustle of a camp and the busy scenes of public life," Washington planned to live out the retirement years of his life.

Not that Mount Vernon offered a life of inactivity without challenges, but Washington thrived on them. He had turned the farm he had inherited from his half brother Lawrence into a productive plantation. Before he brought Martha and her children to live at Mount Vernon in 1759, he added another story to the house's original one and one-half stories. In 1774, he began construction of an addition to the south end of the house that would contain his study and a private bedchamber. From the battlefield he directed the building of a large dining room with a huge Palladian window, on the north end of the mansion. Also added in his absence was the piazza with its eight distinctive square columns, raised in 1777 on the east front. The wide porch, which afforded a panoramic view of the Potomac River and the Maryland shore beyond, was a unique feature among Virginia manor houses. Now home again, Washington busied himself inspecting the additions, deciding on the decoration for his new rooms, and ordering paving stones for the piazza. Most of his day, however, was spent overseeing the work on his four adjoining farms.

Martha's domain included the mansion and dependencies, where the air was pervaded with the aroma of her famous hams hanging in the smokehouse. Guests often remarked that Mount Vernon's many outbuildings, where much plantation activity was centered, gave the appearance of a small village. Washington's census of 1786 showed that 67 slaves labored at the Mansion House Farm. Slaves spent long days at work in the kitchen, the laundry, and in the vegetable and flower gardens. Women could be found spinning and weaving cloth, and men labored in the stable, at the blacksmith forge, and at shoemaking. Industry echoed through the air, from the hammer and anvil to the whir of the spinning wheel. All of this activity undoubtedly caught the attention of Nelly and little Washington.

At Mount Vernon there was a constant parade of visitors — neighbors, relatives and strangers — who came to pay their respects to the hero of the Revolution. In one year alone, Washington recorded that he had welcomed 423 visitors to his home. Hospitality was a long-standing tradition at Mount Vernon. In the summer of 1784, the children and their grandparents welcomed a guest who received more attention than all others, the Marquis de Lafayette. Because of his commitment to liberty, Lafayette, a loyal subject of Louis XVI, had allied himself with a ragged crew of American colonists in dubious battle against a crowned monarch. Although Nelly was only five when the Marquis visited, she was impressed by the great affection her grandfather felt for this Frenchman. Washington considered him a member of his family — the son he never had. Lafayette shared the same warm regard for Washington and had even named his first-born son George Washington Lafayette. Before he arrived, the Marquis had written to his friend, "There is no rest for me till I go to Mount Vernon. I long for the pleasure to embrace you, my dear General; and the happiness of being once more with you will be so great that no words can express it."

During Lafayette's stay, a steady flow of visitors came to honor this charming man from across the Atlantic who had believed in America's independence and had come to her aid. The French general adored America for its example of liberty, and America in turn adored him. When his visit ended,

Washington, to defer their parting, accompanied Lafayette to Annapolis. When he returned to Mount Vernon he wrote a sentimental farewell letter to the Marquis: "In the moment of our separation, upon the road as I have travelled, and every hour since, I have felt all that love, respect, and attachment for you, with which length of years, close connections, and your merits have inspired me." Following her grandfather's example, Nelly came to love the Marquis, and they would carry on a lifelong correspondence in which she always addressed him as "Father."

Although many public and private affairs claimed Washington's attention, he took time out in 1785 to look for a tutor to reside at Mount Vernon to "initiate two little children (a girl of six and a boy of four years of age, descendants of the deceased Mr. Custis, who live with me and are very promising) in the first rudiments of education." The tutor's responsibilities would be light, so the applicant would also take on the duties of Washington's personal secretary, and would "sit at my Table, will live as I live, will mix with the Company who resort to the house, and will be treated in every respect with civility, and proper attention."

The first tutor to instruct the Custis children was William Shaw, but his residence at Mount Vernon was brief. Gideon Snow's short tenure followed. To help find a tutor who would fill the position permanently, Washington enlisted the aid of Noah Webster, the dictionary editor. He wrote to Webster, "I am equally obliged to you, Sir, for your kind assurance of looking out for an Instructor for the little folks of this family."

Tobias Lear arrived at Mount Vernon in 1786 to serve as the children's new tutor. A native of New Hampshire, Lear's credentials included a diploma from Harvard University. He soon became a close friend of Washington and his family, and remained so until the general's death. A few years after his arrival, Tobias Lear wrote of his charges, "A little Grandson of Mrs. Washington's, by a former husband, and his Sister, the one of 6 and the other of 8 years old afford me no small pleasure & amusement in instructing them, they are, without partiality, as fine children as were ever seen, I never thought I could be so much attached to children as I am to them." Lear had also gained the respect of the children's mother, who wrote to him seeking advice on how she could best maintain a relationship with her children without her constant presence.

Nelly's early schooling was not unlike that of most girls of the Virginia gentry. The ability to read, however, put her in the minority of Virginia's females, only 30 percent of whom were literate during the latter half of the 18th century. Nelly studied penmanship and grammar, and she learned to speak with eloquence. French and history were also part of her curriculum. Although Nelly's early education was typical of most children of the planter class, her interest and enthusiasm for learning was not. Lear found that Nelly was an extremely receptive student who needed no prodding. Of her literary accomplishments Nelly later claimed, "I began to repeat & love Poetry before I was five years old." At the age of eight she was reciting passages from the *Iliad,* taught to her by Colonel David Humphreys, Washington's former aide.

In contrast to the successful early education of the Custis grandchildren at Mount Vernon, their older sisters at Abingdon were faring less well. Eleanor Stuart had at first attempted to teach her children reading and writing. But she realized her own inadequacies. Then their stepfather obtained the services of "old Tracy." Eliza wrote of her tutor, "I had no respect for my master, & treated him often with contempt, my sister joined me to torment him, he knew not how to make us respect him." Although Eliza was just as anxious to learn as Nelly, her interests were ignored and even laughed at. "I told them to teach me what they pleased, . . . [but] they would not teach me Greek & Latin because I was a girl. They laughed & said women ought not to know those things, & mending, writing, Arithmetic & Music was all I could be permitted to acquire, I thought of this often with deep regret."

At Mount Vernon, Martha Washington picked up where Tobias Lear left off by teaching her granddaughter how to run a large household. This extensive course of study was the primary curriculum of girls from wealthy southern families. Martha also taught Nelly the arts of embroidery and knitting, and they devoted part of every day to religious study and prayer. The Washingtons had sometimes attended nearby Pohick Church on Sundays, where Washington was a vestryman, but after the Revolution it fell into disuse, and the family worshipped at Christ Church in Alexandria. Needlework and religious devotion, two passions instilled in her by her grandmother, would give Nelly the greatest pleasure and comfort throughout her life. They also brought Martha and her granddaughter closer together. Except for the time spent with her tutor, Nelly was at her grandmother's side for the greater part of the day. A strong emotional bond of dependence grew between the two that Nelly never had a chance to cultivate with her own mother.

Eleanor Stuart's concern about the advantages of Nelly over her older sisters was already proving to be a valid one. Nelly's early training was firmly established. She would one day look back on her early days at Mount Vernon and reflect, "What should I have been if my blessed Grandmother had not early taught me to think and to pray."

"Livelier than, Ever"

*I*n 1787, Washington was appointed a delegate to the Constitutional Convention in Philadelphia by Virginia Governor Edmund Randolph. Washington declined the offer because he had already declared his resignation from public life, and he was happy in his retirement. Fellow Virginian James Madison urged Washington to change his mind. That this body could bring the continent together under a new government seemed a forlorn hope unless Washington took part. Washington reconsidered his attendance at the convention and accepted Robert Morris's invitation to stay in his Philadelphia town house. But he would be coming alone because "Mrs Washington has become too domestick and too attentive to two little Grandchildren to leave home." With Washington serving as president of the convention, state representatives produced a document unlike anything that existed in the world before, a constitution that emphasized liberty and equality. That summer while Washington was in Philadelphia, he ordered the symbolic dove of peace weather vane that would crown the cupola of his mansion. It was his final embellishment to Mount Vernon.

The new U.S. Constitution created the position of chief executive, which was crafted with George Washington in mind. Only he had the respect and strength necessary to bring the country out of the governmental chaos following the Revolution. He was unanimously chosen by the Electoral College on February 4, 1789, and in the spring he received the official notification that he had been elected first President of the United States. Typically, Washington accepted the position with reluctance, having modest doubts of his ability to fulfill it. "My movements to the chair of Government," he wrote, "will be accompanied by feelings not unlike those of a culprit who is going to the place of execution." By answering the call of his country, Washington would once again be taken away from his beloved Mount Vernon.

The president-elect had to borrow money to settle his affairs and pay travel expenses to his own inaugural in the temporary capital of New York. He was officially informed of his election to the presidency on April 14 and two days later he left Mount Vernon, accompanied by his aide David Humphreys and the secretary of Congress, Charles Thomson. Martha and the grandchildren would follow a month later. As Washington rode out through his gates, he undoubtedly glanced back across the bowling green for one last look at his beloved home. His doubts on leaving his home and facing an unknown future are evident in his diary entry for April 16, "About 10 o'clock I bade adieu to Mount Vernon, to private life, and to domestic felicity, and with a mind oppressed with more anxious and painful sensations than I have words to express, set out for New York . . . with the best disposition to render service to my country in obedience to its call, but with less hope of answering its expectations."

At every stop on his week-long journey Washington was heralded with orations, parades and toasts. Flowers were strewn in his path and specially-composed songs were sung in his honor. When Washington arrived in New York Harbor on April 23, the shores were crowded with cheering throngs. "The successive Motion of hats, from the Battery to the Coffee House, was like the rolling motion of the sea, or a field of grain waving with the wind." The president-elect spent a busy week organizing his affairs and preparing for his inauguration. Shortly before 2:00 p.m. on April 30, George Washington, with his hand over his heart, took the oath of office on the balcony of Federal Hall, overlooking Wall Street. The new president was saluted with cheers, pealing bells and a cannonade from the harbor. President

Washington bowed to the crowd and then withdrew to the Senate chamber where he delivered his inaugural address.

Bound for New York, Martha, with Nelly, age 10, and little Washington, age eight, left Mount Vernon on May 16, accompanied by Robert Lewis, who was to serve on his uncle's staff. En route they stopped at Abingdon, where the Custis children were reunited with their family. When it was time for them to continue on to New York, the parting was an emotional one. "The children were a-bawling," wrote Lewis, "and everything [was] in the most lamentable situation." Eliza Custis realized there would now be fewer opportunities to visit her grandparents. She claimed that the election of her grandfather caused "serious injury" to her health, suffering for 21 days afterward with a "nervous fever." The move would have an effect on Nelly and little Washington also. They had never traveled more than 10 or 15 miles from Mount Vernon, and they were familiar only with the slow rhythm of plantation life and not with bustling, crowded cities. A greater distance would now separate them from their mother, forcing the bond between Nelly, little Washington and their grandparents to grow even stronger.

Although the fanfare that greeted the small traveling party was not as great as the veneration Washington had received on his journey to the capital, it was still enough to overwhelm young Nelly. This was the first occasion on which she witnessed the great adulation the people felt for her Grandpapa. Parades, ceremonies and banquets were held in their honor all along the route. At Elizabethtown Point the travelers were met by President Washington, and together they crossed the bay into New York City. The presidential barge was rowed by 13 oarsmen in white uniforms, and 13 guns roared out an earsplitting salute. When the barge docked the enormous crowd called out "God Bless Lady Washington!" to the new president's wife. To Nelly this was a strange greeting for her unpretentious grandmother, who was garbed in simple homespun. Drums rolled, fifes shrilled and military salutes boomed. "Dear little Washington seemed to be lost in a maze at the great parade that was made for us all the way we

come," wrote Martha. As for Nelly, the triumphant procession was
unlike anything she had experienced at Mount Vernon.

Located just a block from the East River at the corners of
Cherry and Queen Streets, the president's house was described as
the grandest house in America. Standing three stories high, the
house appeared to have sufficient rooms for formal receptions
and dinners, bedrooms for the Washington family and their secre-
taries, as well as office space. New York City, with its population
of just over 20,000, was rebuilding from the war, and everywhere
new streets were being laid out, all of them bordered by new
buildings. Lampposts were also being installed. The city's growth
gave evidence that prosperity was in the air. And Nelly was
entranced by the constant activity in the city's streets. Martha
wrote that her granddaughter "spends her time at the window
looking at carriages etc., passing by, which is new to her." But
this preoccupation with city life ended when Nelly returned to
her lessons.

Despite the numerous demands on the new first lady, Martha's
primary concern was to choose appropriate schools for the
grandchildren. New York City offered a variety of rich educational opportunities. Nelly was enrolled in the school of Isabella
Graham at Five Maiden Lane. Mrs. Graham's school was attended
by the daughters of many prominent New York families as well
as the daughters of leading government officials. It was well
known throughout the country, and some of the students came
from as far away as the Carolinas. According to an advertisement,
studies included, "Reading, English, Spelling, and Grammar,
Plainwork, Embroidery, Cloathwork, and various works of fancy,
Writing, Arithmetic, Geography, Drawing, Painting, Japanning,

PASTEL PORTRAIT OF NELLY CUSTIS BY JAMES SHARPLES,
CIRCA 1796. AT THE SAME TIME, THE ARTIST
COMPLETED SIMILAR PORTRAITS OF GEORGE AND MARTHA
WASHINGTON, GEORGE WASHINGTON PARKE CUSTIS,
AND THE MARQUIS DE LAFAYETTE'S SON, GEORGE WASHINGTON
LAFAYETTE, WHO WAS PART OF THE PRESIDENTIAL HOUSEHOLD
WHILE HIS FATHER WAS IMPRISONED IN FRANCE.
MOUNT VERNON LADIES' ASSOCIATION.

Philigree, Music, Dancing, and the French language." The advertisement also boasted that one of Mrs. Graham's assistants was
"for nine years in France" and had assisted in some of the "first
Boarding Schools in London." Nelly started school on November
10, 1789; being a day scholar, she ate her lunch at school.

In the back of her French exercise book, Nelly set down her
own disciplined course of study for learning the language.

> Mondays — Get some French by heart. Rehearse the last two
> grammar lessons.
>
> Wednesdays and Fridays — Get 1 page of Dialogues; get 1/2
> page grammar lessons.
>
> Tuesdays and Thursdays — Get 1 page of Dialogues.
>
> Saturdays — Be examined in the Dialogue and parse some
> French.
>
> Translate every day but Saturday.

Nelly took private piano lessons from Alexander Reinagle, a
prolific composer, who was one of the finest musicians to immi-
grate to America during the 18th century. To teach her in drawing, Nelly turned to William Dunlap, a well-known painter, play-
wright and historian. Painting mostly still lifes such as vases of
flowers and baskets of fruit, she proved to be a talented student.
Obviously, Nelly had some of the best teachers a child could
have. Tobias Lear, who had traded his position as the children's
tutor for that of the principal secretary to the new president,
observed that both Nelly and little Washington had the finest
instructors in the country. Lear took great pride in the fact that he
personally laid the foundation of their education, and he was
pleased that they continued to make good progress.

At first Washington spent about $150 a year on each Custis
child for education and supplies. This increased to $250, and later
$300 per child as they grew older. Whenever money was spent
on the Custis children, it was itemized separately by Washington
in his account book, so that at any time a total of sums that had

been provided for them could be ascertained and charged to
their estates if he desired. But all was not schoolwork, as
Washington's account book proves. Also recorded were admis-
sion fees to New York's delightful entertainments. The children
often went to the theatre, where they saw such comedies as *The
Wonder!* and *The Old Maid.* They visited a museum of "Natural
Curiosities" and went to Mr. Bowen's display of waxworks, where
the exhibits included contemporary subjects such as "The
President of the United States, sitting under a Canopy, in his
Military Dress — Over the Head of his Excellency a Fame is sus-
pended (also in Wax) crowning him with a Wreath of Laurels."
John Fenno's *Gazette of the United States* reported the visit of
Washington and his family to the exhibition.

In February 1790, the presidential household moved to a larger
residence at 39-41 Broadway between Trinity Church and
Bowling Green, where Washington paid $100 monthly rent. By
the end of the year, plans were made to move the nation's capital
to a permanent location. It was decided to lay out the Federal
City along the Potomac River near Georgetown, Virginia. In the
meantime, the capital was temporarily transferred to Philadelphia,
the largest city in America, where the first family moved into the
Robert Morris house on Market and Sixth Streets. Like New York
City, Philadelphia was also experiencing post-Revolution prosperity in the areas of commerce, science and art. The city already
possessed a rich history. The Declaration of Independence had
been signed there 14 years before, and the new Constitution had
been drafted there. Philadelphia's finest buildings were those
devoted to government and religion. Immigrants flocked to the
city to take advantage of Philadelphia's religious tolerance. The
city's port on the Delaware River was one of the nation's busiest,
receiving ships from as far away as China. Philadelphia pulsed
with life, offering a cosmopolitan scene of vendors, shoppers and
entertainers. Fine carriages of the townspeople along with farmers' wagons in from the country blended together, filling the thor-
oughfares. Troops marched on the cobblestones, and ladies and
gentlemen promenaded. Dogs and children frolicked while their

elders went about their work. At night the candles were lit, the taverns were crowded and the parlors of the wealthy were filled with the city's elite.

Tobias Lear reported to Eleanor Stuart on her children's busy life and the benefits they had as members of the presidential household in Philadelphia. Although grateful for news of the children, Eleanor lamented that her two older children did not have the same advantages. Fearful that her young son might forget her, she implored Lear to "shake hands with my Dear Boy . . . don't let him forget he has a mother." Nelly, at age 11, began to attend her first balls and parties. Understandably, her letters to her sisters back home in Virginia were filled with more details of her social activities than her academic progress. Her mother wrote Lear: "I am much alarm'd about My Dear Nelly. From her letters to her Sisters she appears too much engaged in dissapation. My Dear little artless child will I much fear soon be an affected, trifling, Miss of the Town. She is too young to be admitted to Ball & Tea Parties. In a few Months I suppose she will be taught to listen to every Fop. These were my fears when she left Me. Tell Me my Friend what can I, what ought I to do?" She concluded, "Her Dear Grandmama is too much pleased with the attentions paid to Nelly to judge of their impropriety."

Tobias Lear agreed that Martha was spoiling Nelly and her brother. In fact, Lear wrote that little Washington was not to be scolded because the president knew that any severe disciplining of the boy would upset his Grandmama. As for Nelly, Martha described her granddaughter as "a little wild creature," and added, "I hope when Nelly has a little more gravatie she will be a good girl, — At present — she is I fear half crazey." Later in her life, Nelly recalled that Eliza Powel, a frequent visitor to the Washington household, had commented about her disheveled attire saying, "You look as if your clothes were thrown on with a Pitchfork!" Reflecting on that incident, Nelly agreed: "I was always too restless to take time & pains in dressing — If covered modestly, & clean, I cared for nothing else." Most visitors to the president's house agreed that Nelly's vibrant energy was part of her charm.

Although the Washingtons' personal tastes were simple, they entertained officially with stately elegance to show the world that the head of their new country was due as much respect as that accorded European monarchs. President Washington had formal levees for political officials and men of distinction on Tuesday afternoons from 3:00 p.m. to 4:00 p.m. This gave gentlemen a chance to meet the president at his home and to exchange a few words with him. The first lady had receptions, or drawing rooms, on Friday evenings at 8:00 p.m. Although Martha's receptions were similar to the president's, the first lady's were more sociable.

Abigail Adams, wife of the vice president, who had traveled with her husband when he was the foreign minister to Great Britain and was familiar with the royal method of holding court, described one of Martha's receptions in a letter to her sister: "The form of Reception is this, the servants announce and Col. Humphries and Mr Lear, receives every Lady at the door, and Hands her up to Mrs. Washington to whom she makes a most Respectfull courtesy and then is seated without noticing any of the rest of the company. The President then comes up and speaks to the Lady, which he does with a grace and dignity and ease, that leaves Royal George far behind him." Abigail had high praise for the president's wife as well: "Mrs. Washington is a most friendly, good Lady, always plesent & easy, doatingly fond of her Grandchildren, to whom she is quite the Grandmama . . . . She is plain in her dress, but that plainness is the best of every article . . . . Her manners are modest and unassuming, dignified and feminine . . . . No lady can be more deservedly beloved and esteemed as she is . . . . I found myself more deeply impressed than I ever did before their Majesties of Britain."

If only Nelly had written a description of one particular evening's reception! The ostrich feathers in the headdress worn by a young female guest brushed against a chandelier and caught fire, but Major William Jackson, one of the president's young aides, prevented a disaster by quickly extinguishing the flames with his bare hands before anyone was injured.

The first family was not only seen at the president's levees and the first lady's receptions. Less official family activities were often visible to the citizens of Philadelphia. On Saturday afternoon they could be seen leisurely riding around the city in their cream-colored coach. The excursions offered Washington relaxation away from his presidential duties and an opportunity for Martha and the children to be a part of the city's vigorous life. They were often accompanied by Nelly's pet, a green parrot that she was teaching to sing in French. Martha and the children also visited Charles Willson Peale's museum of "Natural Curiosities." Peale, a portrait artist and scientist, opened the first public museum in the world that included displays of fossils and stuffed animals. The first lady and her granddaughter shopped together at Mr. Whiteside's fancy new dry goods shop, where Martha bought Nelly a spangled dress for dancing school and paintbrushes for her drawing class. In the evenings, the Washingtons and the children occasionally attended the South Street Theatre, where an east stage box was set aside for the president and his family. On Sundays they went to Christ Church on Second and Market Streets.

At the age of 12, Nelly became friends with Elizabeth Bordley, daughter of John Beale Bordley, whom Washington had appointed to receive subscriptions to the bank of the United States. The two young girls began a friendship that would last for over 61 years. When the girls were separated at the end of Washington's presidential term, the friendship continued through a voluminous correspondence, creating one of the finest collections of letters between two female friends of the late 18th and early 19th centuries. Nelly often gave glimpses into life at Mount Vernon during Washington's final years. She recorded momentous occasions, trivial news, sorrows and joys. In their last days Nelly reflected on the bygone years they had shared together in Philadelphia, "where the Sun always appears to shine as it did in our hearts in those happy days."

Elizabeth often spent Saturdays with Nelly playing in the attic of the president's house, where, along with their other playmates, they put on amateur theatricals. They called themselves the Young American Company. As a result of their devotion to one another, Elizabeth Bordley was the most privileged witness of the habits of the presidential family. Her writings include the description of a private moment in the Washington home. During the presidential years Martha retired to her room at an early hour, unless detained by company. Nelly always accompanied her. Miss Bordley wrote:

> One evening my father's carriage was late in coming for me, and my dear young friend invited me to accompany her to her grandmama's room. There, after some little chat, Mrs. Washington apologized to me for pursuing her usual preparations for the night, and Nelly entered upon her accustomed duty by reading a chapter and psalm from the old family Bible, after which all present knelt in evening prayer; Mrs. Washington's faithful maid then sang a verse of some soothing hymn, and leaning down, received the parting blessing for the night, with some emphatic remarks on her duties, improvements, etc. The effect of these habits and teachings appeared in the granddaughter's character through life.

In March 1793, all of Washington's grandchildren were present at the simple ceremony in the Senate Chamber that marked his second inauguration. Eliza and Martha Custis had come from Virginia to see their grandfather take the oath of office for the second time. Tobias Lear remarked that Eliza and Martha " . . . are fine girls. I think it is much to be lamented that they . . . should be so much secluded from society." Dr. Stuart, who Eliza described as having become a "gloomy mortal," had moved his family to Hope Park, which his stepdaughter complained "had nothing to recommend it," being located 20 miles from Alexandria. But for the time being, the Custis girls could enjoy the benefits of society in the capital city. And they were happy to be in the company of their grandparents again, particularly their Grandmama, whom Eliza loved "more than my mother." When they left for home Eliza's "heart broke."

That summer one of the most horrifying epidemics in America's history infected Philadelphia. On the wings of mosquitoes from the waterfront, yellow fever swept across the capital city, killing 4,000 inhabitants, leaving the skin of its victims deep yellow or black. Nelly described the fever as "that destructive evil." The epidemic swept through the city streets, touching almost every household as the body count mounted. Nine died on August 1, 12 on the 7th, 11 on the 13th, 24 on the 28th. By September the death toll climbed as high as 40 or 50 per day. Blacks, who were thought to be immune to the disease, drove wagons up and down the city streets, and hollered, "Bring out your dead." Martha feared for the children, but would not leave Philadelphia without her husband. The president, realizing that his presence offered hope to a city that was paralyzed with fear, refused to leave for Mount Vernon until September 10. After a restful stay of seven-and-a-half weeks on the banks of the Potomac, the family moved to the Isaac House in Germantown, northwest of Philadelphia, where they waited for the epidemic to subside.

When they returned to the president's house in November, Nelly resumed her piano lessons with Alexander Reinagle, who had also moved from New York to Philadelphia. James Robardet and a Mr. Cenas instructed her in dance. Henry Capron taught her on her new pear-shaped guitar, purchased for her by her grandfather. Capron advertised, "At two lessons per week he engages to perfect any person, possessing a tolerable ear, in the space of six months." In two large volumes, using her elaborate script, Nelly copied all of her favorite musical compositions. Her collection included the works of Mozart, Haydn, Beethoven, and Handel, musicians who represented what was then the height of the classical period in Europe. Among her music was a number of selections that paid homage to her grandfather, including "General Washington's March," the "President's March," and the "Faederal March."

Nelly enjoyed singing as well. On one occasion, she sent a note to the home of her friend Elizabeth Bordley requesting her "to take tea with me tomorrow evening — we expect Mrs Murray & Mrs McHenry to tea, & I wish very much that they should hear you sing our Duett —." Her vocal pieces included songs from the operas *Rosina, The Poor Soldiers,* and *The Pirates.* In her copy of the song "William and Ann" there appeared the line "and vindicate the British name." Nelly struck through the word "British" and wrote "American."

NELLY CUSTIS'S HARPSICHORD OCCUPIES A
PLACE OF HONOR IN THE LITTLE PARLOR AT MOUNT VERNON.
GEORGE WASHINGTON ORDERED THE INSTRUMENT FROM LONDON FOR THE
PRESIDENTIAL HOUSEHOLD IN PHILADELPHIA IN 1793. THE
HARPSICHORD RETURNED TO MOUNT VERNON WITH
THE FAMILY IN 1797 AT THE END OF WASHINGTON'S PRESIDENCY. YEARS LATER,
THE HARPSICHORD WAS THE FIRST PIECE OF ORIGINAL
FURNITURE TO BE RETURNED TO MOUNT VERNON AFTER THE MOUNT VERNON
LADIES' ASSOCIATION PURCHASED THE HOME IN 1858.
MOUNT VERNON LADIES' ASSOCIATION.

"Grandmamma always spoilt Washington." Nelly believed that Martha tipped the scale of indulgence in her brother's favor. But as for her grandfather, Nelly wrote, "He liked me to ask him for all that I wished to have and never refused me anything." Whether she asked for it or not, in December 1793, Washington purchased for her a musical instrument that is more associated with Nelly Custis than any other artifact at Mount Vernon. A beautiful harpsichord, costing Washington 21 pounds, seven shillings and five pence, ordered from the London firm of Longman & Broderip, was delivered to the president's house. Although she would become an accomplished player of the instrument and would spend many happy times at its dual keyboards, these results did not come about without some struggle. Martha saw to it that Nelly practiced from four to five hours a day. "As to the story of Nelly Custis, my sister, practising very long and very unwillingly at the harpsichord," her brother remembered, "that part of the tale . . . is true. The poor girl would play and cry, and cry and play, for long hours under the immediate eye of her grandmother." Thomas Jefferson sometimes brought his daughter Polly to practice with Nelly.

Washington seems to have purchased the harpsichord as much for his own pleasure as for Nelly's. Washington said he could neither sing "nor raise a single note on any instrument." But he enjoyed spending an evening listening to Nelly play, and occasionally he suggested what pieces to purchase from the musical catalogues she received. Nelly was Washington's pet. He loved her company, her gaiety, and her intelligence. He liked to see Nelly and her friends "happy and gay." But Nelly lamented that "his presence chilled my young companions and his own relatives feared to speak or laugh before him — this was occasioned by the awe and respect he inspired." Of her own relationship with her Grandpapa she wrote, "I have often made him laugh heartily at the relation of my frolics and difficulties . . . . I have never felt that awe of him which others did."

Nelly also adopted all of her grandfather's political beliefs, and she was not afraid to speak her opinions. The factionalism in

NELLY CUSTIS AND GEORGE WASHINGTON PARKE CUSTIS JOINED GEORGE
AND MARTHA WASHINGTON FOR A FORMAL PORTRAIT BY
EDWARD SAVAGE IN 1796, DURING WASHINGTON'S SECOND AND FINAL
PRESIDENTIAL TERM. MRS. WASHINGTON POINTS WITH HER FAN TO A MAP OF
THE "CAPITAL CITY," THEN BEING DEVELOPED ON THE
BANKS OF THE POTOMAC RIVER, 16 MILES FROM MOUNT VERNON.
NATIONAL GALLERY OF ART, WASHINGTON.
ANDREW W. MELLON COLLECTION.

Washington's cabinet was a thorn in his side throughout his administration. Alexander Hamilton, the secretary of the treasury, represented the Federalists who supported industry and a strong central government dominated by propertied men. Thomas Jefferson's Antifederalists believed that the nation's future prosperity lay in remaining agrarian, with strength based upon small farmers and not on a powerful central government. Jefferson criticized the formalities Washington brought to the presidency, claiming the ceremonies resembled a monarchy. Washington ignored his critics, but Nelly resented any criticism of her grandfather or his administration. And she never forgave Jefferson or the Antifederalist party. She described herself as having become "an outrageous politician, perfectly *federal.*"

Nelly was frequently called upon to entertain her Grandpapa's friends, who gathered at the president's house most evenings. Her outgoing personality charmed them all, and her gaiety only thinly masked her intelligence. When she was seated at her harpsichord, the soft candlelight illuminated her long auburn hair and fair complexion, captivating her guests. But the feeling was not necessarily mutual. Before one evening's entertainment she wrote to Elizabeth Bordley, "We have a large company of the *Honorable Congress* to dine with us, & I must not be so remiss to go out in the evening as they like to hear musick although they do not know one note from another." Her association with serious politicians did not diminish her high spirits. She wore a pink and white turban on many of these occasions, and according to a guest, Nelly was "livelier than ever."

In January 1795, Nelly traveled to Alexandria to attend the wedding of her sister, Martha Parke Custis. Martha, who was described as being the most like her grandmother of all the Custis children, was to marry Thomas Peter, the son of a prosperous Georgetown merchant. Nelly stayed with the Stuarts at Hope Park, which was undoubtedly crowded. Even though she was in ill health following the births of both Nelly and George Washington Parke Custis, Eleanor had an additional 16 children by Dr. Stuart. Ignoring the ordeal of Eleanor's pregnancies, Tobias Lear quipped, "Mr. Stuart goes on in the usual way producing a new inhabitant to the United States every year."

Nelly served as her sister's bridesmaid and wore a new dress and her grandmother's watch. She took part in all of the wedding festivities. The 15-year-old Nelly attended a ball in Georgetown, evidently this time with the permission of her mother, where she met many young suitors. But Nelly said she "was in no danger of being captivated by any one here." She described the ball in a detailed letter to her grandfather in Philadelphia. In his reply Washington commented that she wrote "a fair hand" and her "ideas are lively and your descriptions agreeable." He advised her to begin a new paragraph when she changed the subject. And perhaps feeling that his granddaughter's distance placed her out of his protection, he took the opportunity to include some father-ly advice on choosing a suitor with caution:

> A hint here; men and women feel the same inclinations to each other now that they always have done, and which they will continue to do until there is a new order of things, and you, as others have done, may find, perhaps, that the passions of your sex are easier raised than allayed. Do not therefore boast too soon or too strongly of your insensibility to, or resis-tance of, its powers . . . . When the fire is beginning to kindle, and your heart growing warm, propound these questions to it. Who is this invader? Have I a competent knowledge of him? Is he a man of good character; a man of sense? For, be assured, a sensible woman can never be happy with a fool. What has been his walk in life? Is he a gambler, a spendthrift, or a drunkard? Is his fortune sufficient to maintain me in the man-ner I have been accustomed to live, and my sisters do live, and is he one to whom my friends can have no reasonable objection? . . Have I sufficient ground to conclude that his affections are engaged to me?

He concluded by warning that "a thorough-paced coquette dies in celebacy."

After the marriage of her younger sister Martha, Eliza Custis began to worry she would never fall in love. Washington wrote her some advice as well. In a letter to Eliza he attempted to erase any romantic notions she had about courtship. "Do not in your contemplation of the marriage state, look for felicity before you consent to wed," he wrote. "Whatever may be your first impression of the man, it will end in disappointment . . . all our enjoyments fall short of our experience." Eliza would one day learn for herself the truth of Washington's words. Shortly after she received the letter, however, she met and became engaged to Thomas Law. Law was a wealthy Englishman who made his fortune in India and was now speculating in real estate in the new Federal City. Eliza was 19 years old to Law's 40.

During autumn 1795, the Washingtons sojourned at Mount Vernon. It was an uneasy stay for Nelly, because she dreaded her upcoming separation from her grandmother in order to spend the winter and spring with her mother at Hope Park and attend Eliza's wedding in March. The stay was Martha's idea. She believed that it was "proper and necessary" for Nelly to spend the winter with her mother, whom she had seen little of since Washington had become president. Nelly wrote to Elizabeth Bordley, "To part from Grandmama is all I dread . . . It is impossible to love any one, more than I love her, & it will grieve me extremely to part from her."

After Nelly had gone to Hope Park and Martha had returned to Philadelphia, Nelly found the separation to be just as difficult as she had imagined. Again she confided her feelings to her friend Elizabeth Bordley, "I have gone through the greatest trial, I ever experienced — parting with my beloved Grandmama — this is the first separation for any time since I was two years old. Since my father's death she has been even more than a Mother to me, and the President the most affectionate of Fathers. I love them more than any one — You can guess then how severely I must feel this parting, even for a short time."

Compared to the activity of the capital city, life at Hope Park seemed slow and withdrawn. Eleanor Stuart realized that her daughter was having difficulty adjusting, and she knew there were "so many enchanting circumstances" to make Nelly prefer to be with her grandmother in Philadelphia, but she appreciated the fact that Nelly was "so chearfully submitting to the retired life" she led with her mother. In fact, the "retired life" at the

Stuart home prepared Nelly for the day when she would leave the city of Philadelphia and return to Mount Vernon. Nelly recognized a change in herself. "I am grown very industrious — & shall shortly be grave as any quaker, or baptist of your acquaintance," she reported to Elizabeth. Several months later, just before her 17th birthday, she concluded a letter by saying that from now on she wanted to be called Eleanor. "Nelly is extremely homely in my opinion."

Martha wrote letters to Nelly keeping her informed about life in Philadelphia. The letters were often filled with admonitions about her dress and manners, and when Nelly wrote that she was attending a ball, Martha answered somewhat sourly, "[I] wish you may have as much pleasure as you expect — going to these places one always expects more pleasure than they realize after the matter is over." Eliza's wedding to Thomas Law in March of 1796 was private "without any dancing or parties of any kind," Nelly wrote, sounding disappointed. By May, she looked forward to her reunion with her grandmother. "I wish more & more every day to see her. We have been seperated now near seven months, & that is very long for a first seperation."

In April, when the Washingtons arrived at Mount Vernon, Nelly rushed to meet them, and was introduced to George Washington Lafayette, who had come to temporarily live with the Washingtons. His father, the Marquis de Lafayette, had fought for liberty in the American Revolution and had returned to France to establish it in his native country. When the Bastille, a symbol of despotism, was torn down, Lafayette sent Washington the key to the prison's main door as a tribute from "a Missionary of Liberty to its Patriarch." But the constitutional monarchy crumbled into a reign of terror. Revolutionaries randomly guillotined members of the royal court and their aristocratic friends. The Marquis was exiled for five years. Lafayette's wife sent their son to George Washington for protection, knowing of the special bond between her husband and the president. The young man remained with the Washingtons until November 1797. George Lafayette and Nelly became close friends, and she always referred to him affectionately as her brother.

With Nelly's return to Mount Vernon and her reunion with her grandparents, her former energy and high spirits were restored. "I am as happy as a mortal can wish to be . . . I ride on Horseback — walk, read, write french — work, play & sing & always think the weeks go off too fast." Even a fall from a horse, from which she "never felt the least inconvenience," could not dull her excitement at being back home with her family.

Mount Vernon had much the same curative powers on Washington. With less than one year left of his presidency, he looked forward to his second retirement at Mount Vernon. He wrote to Dr. Stuart, "I can truly say I had rather be at home at Mount Vernon with a friend or two about me, than to be attended at the seat of government by the officers of State and the representatives of every power of Europe."

Washington's second presidential term came to an end in 1797. The celebration of the general's birthday in February had become an annual event, and a final birthnight ball was held at the president's house. It would be the last such event attended by Washington in Philadelphia. The president was host to 1,200 guests who came to bid farewell to him and the first family. On March 4, 1797, the Washingtons attended the inauguration of John Adams as the new president and Thomas Jefferson as vice president. One observer noted that during the latter's taking of the oath Nelly was "terribly agitated."

Amidst the chaos of moving Washington complained, "On one side I am called upon to remember the parrot; on the other to remember the dog. For my part, I would not pine much if both were forgot." Just before her 18th birthday, Nelly said good-bye to Philadelphia and to her dear friend Elizabeth Bordley. On the journey home, Nelly wrote that there were "no adventures of any kind," that is except for the "light Horse of Delaware, & Maryland, who insisted upon attending us through their states, all the Inhabitants of Baltimore who came out to *see*, & *be seen* & to Welcome My Dear Grandpapa — some in carriages, some on Horseback, the others on foot — The gentlemen of George Town also attended us to the River, & four of them rowed us over in a barge." The Washingtons had dinner at Eliza and Thomas Law's house, and lodged for one night at Martha and Thomas Peter's house in Georgetown. Washington was careful to divide his time equally between Nelly's older sisters in order to show no favoritism. The following morning they left for home. The seven-day journey from Philadelphia ended at the gates of Mount Vernon on March 15, 1797. "No consideration under heaven that I can foresee," vowed Washington, "shall again withdraw me from the walks of private life."

"One of those Celestial, Beings"

*L*ike her grandfather, Nelly Custis also looked forward to returning to the banks of the Potomac and the house she loved. Now that she was home she wrote, "Since I left Philadelphia everything has appeared to be a dream, I can hardly realise my *being here*, & that Grandpapa is no longer in office . . . for although I shall ever remember my friends with regret yet I am delighted to be once more settled here, & surrounded by my Dearest relatives." She moved back into the southwest bedroom off the upstairs hall, where her walls were covered with paper painted a bright shade of Prussian blue and were adorned with engravings and a sampling of her own artwork. A corner fireplace added to the room's warmth in winter. Although her bedroom was one of the smallest of the second floor rooms, Nelly said that she "never found it too small, or too close." In fact, she later wrote that she "prefer'd a room in my Beloved Grandmama's house, to a Palace away from her." Nelly continued to spend much of her time with Martha. She assisted with household chores, which included overseeing the work of servants in

PORTRAIT OF ELEANOR PARKE LEWIS,
ATTRIBUTED TO JAMES SHARPLES, *CIRCA* 1800.
*COURTESY OF WOODLAWN PLANTATION, A PROPERTY OF THE
NATIONAL TRUST FOR HISTORIC PRESERVATION.*

the house, kitchen and laundry, and she planned menus and copied recipes. Hours were spent contentedly plying needles threaded with colorful yarns through canvas stretched on wooden frames. And grandmother and granddaughter continued to set aside a portion of each day for religious devotions.

Martha's spirits were also restored by being home again. "I cannot tell you, my dear friend, how much I enjoy home after having been deprived of one so long," she wrote to a friend in Philadelphia, "for our dwelling in New York and Philadelphia was not home, only a sojourning . . . . Nelly and I are companions. Mrs. Law and Mrs. Peters, Nelly's older sisters, are often with us . . . . I am again fairly settled down to the pleasant duties of an old-fashioned Virginia housekeeper, steady as a clock, busy as a bee, and cheerful as a cricket." With every passing year Nelly gained more and more respect for her grandmother.

Nelly sensed her grandfather's relief in having the burdens of the presidency lifted from his shoulders. Now he could return to his greatest pleasure, that of overseeing his estate. Mount Vernon was always healing to Washington, never as an easy retreat, but healing as a congenial enterprise, each day brimming with problems he loved to meet, profits he longed to make, filled with nature and weather, crops, animals and men. When Washington arrived home he found that his mansion and farms had suffered from neglect during the eight years of his presidency and needed his immediate attention. He set about putting the house in order and wrote, "We are in a litter and dirt, occassioned by joiners, masons, and painters working in the house, all parts of which, as well as the outbuildings, I find upon examination to be exceedingly out of repairs . . . . "

"Grandpapa is very well, & has already turned Farmer again," Nelly wrote. And in his fields Washington found another challenge. Mount Vernon's soil had always been at best mediocre. The nutrients had been drained from the soil as a result of many years of cultivation. When Washington had grown tobacco he was never able to duplicate his neighbors in quality or quantity. So he switched to cultivating wheat and corn. But even though it was one of his two principal crops, Washington had been forced to buy corn in 1786 in order to feed his laborers and livestock. In an effort to make his farms more lucrative, he had ordered a book for his library entitled *A New System of Agriculture, or a Speedy Way to Grow Rich,* and he also adopted the methods of Arthur Young, the great English agronomist. Washington changed his technique by sowing his fields in grasses rather than permitting them to lie fallow between harvest and the next planting. Nevertheless, Washington often made more money from his fisheries located on the Potomac River and his mill on Dogue Run than he did from farming.

Nelly wrote to Elizabeth Bordley describing a typical day during Washington's retirement years.

One day in retirement was the history of his whole domestic life. He rose before sunrise, always wrote or read until 7 in summer or half past seven in winter. His breakfast was then ready — he ate three small mush cakes (Indian meal) swimming in butter and honey, drank three cups of tea without cream — after breakfast retired to his room if alone — if he had company to the drawing room — at 9 he rode to his farm until 2 — then dressed for dinner, at 3 he dined, always preferred plain roast or boiled and an Indian cake. After dinner he drank 3 glasses of madiera. Late a small plate of Indian walnuts. In the afternoon he remained with his company or if alone retired to his library — at sunset in summer and at candlelight in winter tea was brought in, after tea he remained with us until 9 — if any ceremonious company were at Mt. Vn. until 10. He generally wrote or read an hour in his room and then retired to bed.

One tradition began in the president's house in Philadelphia and continued during Washington's years of retirement. Nelly spent most evenings entertaining the family by singing or playing on her harpsichord. No longer did she need to be forced to practice or play. Now she truly loved the time after the sun had set and the candles were lit when the family gathered in the little parlor where her harpsichord now stood. But her brief concerts were incomplete. She wrote to Elizabeth Bordley saying she wished "every day to sing duetts," but without her friend "I am obliged to confine myself entirely to Solo's."

The "wild creature" with the disheveled clothing and the singing parrot was replaced by a beautiful, charming, intelligent young lady. As a result of her advantages growing up in the Washington household, Nelly had become one of the most accomplished young women in America. Martha felt enormous pride in her granddaughter, and Nelly made every effort to please the woman to whom she was so devoted.

Visitors to Washington's home were always plentiful. "I have no objection," he wrote, "to any sober or orderly persons gratifying their curiosity in viewing the buildings, Gardens &ct. about Mount Vernon." And come they did, which once prompted Washington to describe Mount Vernon as "a well resorted tavern." Many of the visitors praised Nelly, confirming the fact that she had indeed profited by the direction she had received from her grandmother. She carried off her social duties with ease. She entertained guests on the harpsichord or engaged them in conversation, even attempting to speak in their native language, be it Italian, Spanish or French. Sometimes she amused them by cutting their silhouette. And when they left, they recorded in their journals and letters extravagant praise for Miss Eleanor Parke Custis.

Joshua Brooks, a 25-year-old visitor to Mount Vernon who was introduced to Nelly by Tobias Lear, wrote a vivid description of her. "She appeared to be about twenty, dressed in white sprig muslin tied around her waist with a sky-blue cord with six round balls at the end, head-dress fillet round her head and hair hanging down in ringlets between three turns of her fillet; no powder, about 5 ft 4 high, middling stature and size. Silk stockings. Black shoes with large roses. She appeared modest, well-bred, intelligent, and sensible, has a piercing eye, grecian nose, made judicious remarks and conversed with propriety."

After his stay at Mount Vernon where Nelly presented him
with his cipher composed of flowers, Count Julian Ursyn
Niemcewicz, a Polish poet, lavishly paid tribute to his young
hostess. "She was one of those celestial beings so rarely produced by nature, sometimes dreamed of by poets and painters,
which one cannot see without a feeling of ecstasy. Her sweetness
equals her beauty, and that is perfect. She has many accomplish-

BENJAMIN HENRY LATROBE, A VISITOR TO MOUNT VERNON IN 1796,
CAPTURED A SCENE OF DOMESTIC TRANQUILITY AS THE
WASHINGTONS TOOK TEA ON THE PIAZZA. HIS ELEGANT RENDITION OF
NELLY CUSTIS DEPICTED THE TEENAGER IN A CLASSICAL POSE
AGAINST ONE OF THE PIAZZA'S COLUMN.
MOUNT VERNON LADIES' ASSOCIATION.

ments. She plays the piano, she sings and designs better than the usual woman of America, or even Europe."

Benjamin Latrobe, architect and builder of the new Federal City, complimented Washington and his home, but saved his most generous and effusive flattery for Nelly. "Miss Eleanor Custis . . . has more perfection of form, of expression, of color, of softness, and of firmness of mind than I have ever seen before or conceived consistent with mortality. She is everything that the chissel of Phidias aimed at but could not reach, and the soul beaming through the countenance and glowing in her smile is as superior to her face as mind is to matter." He sketched the young beauty having tea with her family on the piazza. Latrobe's rendering of Nelly with her classical dress and long flowing hair gave her the appearance of a Greek goddess.

Obviously Nelly could have had many suitors had she wished them. But she continued to resist falling in love, knowing that marriage would inevitably separate her from her grandparents. Nelly's would-be suitors were mostly worldly men, many of whom lived in places far from the Washingtons, Mount Vernon and Virginia. George Washington Lafayette was one such person. When a newspaper reporter suggested an impending union between them, Nelly was indignant. The betrothal of the son of the French general and the granddaughter of the father of America was only in the romantic imagination of the reporter. The tradition of the media's exploitation of the first family appears to have begun with Nelly. Given her determination not to relinquish her affections to anyone but her grandparents, Nelly was anxious to deny the rumor, and she wrote to Miss Bordley,

> I wish the world would not be so extremely busy, & impertinent. E P Custis desires not its notice, & would thank those meddling *reporters* never to mention her name — I wish they would also allow her to *marry who* she *pleases* . . . . I shall ever feel an interest & sincere regard for *my young adopted Brother* — but as to being *in love with him* it is entirely out of the question — therefore *I shall certainly never* be *engaged* or

married to him — as whoever is my Husband I must first love him with all my Heart — that is not romantically, but esteem and prefer him before all others, that Man I am not yet acquainted with — perhaps never may be, if so — then I remain E P Custis Spinster for life.

In letters that she told her friend to read and then burn, Nelly was not charitable when describing the local suitors whom she rejected. One young man she said had a "pug nose" and an "ugly mouth." He was a "disagreeable fop" and resembled "a spaniel." Another was "a little milk & water monkey." Charles Carroll, Jr. of Carrollton, Maryland, son of a signer of the Declaration of Independence, came a-wooing, but after dancing with him until 1:00 a.m. at the Union Tavern in Georgetown, Nelly rejected him, saying he had been "too often told of his merit & accomplishments." She described his "personal attractions" as "not very great." A rumor that Nelly had become engaged to Carroll reached her brother at school in Annapolis. He wrote home sending his best wishes to the couple. But George Washington responded, "Young Mr. C. came here about a fortnight ago to dinner, and left us the next morning at breakfast. If his object was such as you say has been reported, it was not declared here; and therefore, the less said upon the subject, particularly by your sister's friends, the more prudent it will be, until the subject develops more." Nelly corroborated Washington's story in a letter to Elizabeth Bordley. "Mr Carroll was at Mount Vernon in March staid one day & night, nothing more than common civility passed on either side, & he marched off as he came since when I have neither seen him, or heard anything of his movements." Charles Carroll eventually became an alcoholic who was unable to control his drinking despite the pleas of his family who, evidently, gave him no sympathy. His wife and daughters left him, and his nephew wrote, "We can't get him to shoot himself, so must bear with this degradation still longer."

George Washington Parke Custis seemed to be headed for a similar fate, one that was common among young male descendants of America's founding fathers, who had a difficult time measuring up to the high standards set by their families. Like his father had been, Custis was a trial to his grandfather and his teachers. After Custis was enrolled in Princeton, Washington wrote Dr. Smith, the college's president, "From his infancy I have discovered in him an almost unconquerable disposition to indolence in everything that did not tend to his amusements; and have exhorted him in the most parental and friendly manner to devote his time to more useful pursuits." Dr. Smith was also unsuccessful at turning Custis into a scholar. The young man was then sent to St. John's College at Annapolis. But after one term he returned to Mount Vernon. Custis's exasperated guardian sent him back to his mother and stepfather at Hope Park, saying, "He appears to me to be moped and stupid, says nothing, and is always in some hole or corner excluded from the company."

Unlike her brother, Nelly's life was soon to follow a more direct course as a result of the arrival at Mount Vernon of Lawrence Lewis, the son of Washington's sister. Betty Lewis looked "so strikingly like her brother, that it was a matter of frolic to throw a cloak around her, and placing a military hat on her head, such was her amazing resemblance that on her appearance battalions would have presented arms and senates risen to do honor to the chief." Her husband Fielding Lewis had gone bankrupt financing the Revolution and had died just after the surrender at Yorktown. For the next 13 years, Betty cared for 11 children and what was left of her dead husband's estate. In the spring of 1797, she caught a cold superintending millwork during a storm and died at her daughter's home. Since the death of her husband, Betty had depended on her son Lawrence to oversee the Lewis farms. After her death, the farms were divided among her children, and Lawrence was no longer needed as their manager.

At the time, George Washington was looking for a secretary to attend to his papers and his many guests, and he felt responsible for employing Lawrence, although he recognized that his nephew was not overly ambitious. But the young man could at least help relieve Washington of the burden of entertaining the many visitors who came to call at Mount Vernon. Washington wrote his nephew, "As both your aunt and I are in the decline of life, and regular in our habits, especially in our hours of rising and going to bed, I require some person (fit and Proper) to ease me of the trouble of entertaining company, particularly of nights, as it is my inclination to retire . . . . either to bed, or to my study, soon after candle-light. In taking these duties (which hospitality obliges me to bestow on company) off my hands, it would render me a very acceptable service." Lawrence agreed to come to his uncle's aid and make Mount Vernon his home. In the late fall of 1797, Nelly wrote to Elizabeth Bordley, "We expect Mr. Lewis, a nephew of the President's to spend the winter here."

Major Lawrence Lewis was a serious, reserved widower whose first wife, Susanna Edmundson, had died in childbirth in 1790, after only one year of marriage. Lawrence had served as an aide-de-camp to General Daniel Morgan in suppressing the Whiskey Rebellion in western Pennsylvania during the second term of Washington's presidency. In every way Lawrence was the antithesis of Nelly, who was 12 years his junior. At the same time, he was the one person Nelly could safely marry and still remain close to the Washingtons. Lawrence was not a world traveler, was not a resident of a distant country and was not interested in straying far from rural Virginia, a sentiment shared by Nelly. "I always have & do now, prefer the Country infinitely, & particularly this place to all others in the world," she wrote. After a year together at Mount Vernon, Nelly realized the benefits of Lawrence's contentment to remain in the employment of his uncle. Lawrence in turn was captivated by Nelly's charismatic energy, a quality which he himself lacked. A serious love affair developed between them.

The relationship reached fruition at the end of 1798 while Washington was in Philadelphia organizing the army for a confrontation with France. America's relationship with France had deteriorated during the French Revolution, and President John Adams had again called Washington out of retirement when he appointed him lieutenant general and commander of the U.S. military forces. Washington was angered by French attacks on

American shipping, and he supported Adams's intention to prepare for war. So Washington once again put down his plow to raise an army, in case fighting was necessary. Lawrence Lewis and George Washington Parke Custis also received commissions. Not to be out-done, Nelly proposed to Elizabeth Bordley the idea of starting their own corps of patriotic, independent female volunteers:

> We shall have black helmets, or morrocco leather, ornamented with black bugles, & an immense Plume of black feathers. you have no idea how becoming it will be . . . Think child how glorious to be celebrated as the preservers of our *Friends & Country.* "In such a cause a Womans vengeance tow'rs above her sex!" — We shall perform wonders I am sure, & our fame will be transmitted to latest posterity.

Hostility between the countries cooled, and armies, both real and imaginary, were unnecessary. Shortly after Washington's return, Nelly wrote that her "Grandpa, Mr Lewis & Mr Lear were taken sick — very dangerously ill, I being *deputy Doctor* had my *hands* full generally, & my *Heart* constantly filled with uneasiness on their accounts." Her anxious feelings about her patients are easy to understand when one remembers the importance of these three men in her life.

The year 1799 began with Washington proclaiming his inno-cence concerning the relationship that had suddenly sprung up between Nelly and Lawrence. He wrote to his brother-in-law, Bartholomew Dandridge, that the romance had developed "with-out my having the smallest suspicion that such an affair was in agitation." But Nelly showed a surprising willingness to divulge to her grandfather the private details of her romance. She related that her Grandpapa "was very curious about all my love letters" and "I showed him all I received from Mr. L."

In February, Nelly informed her friend Elizabeth of the events of the past couple of months in a letter that began with lightness of heart and humor. "Cupid, a small mischievous Urchin, who has been trying sometime to humble my pride, took me by surprise,"

she wrote. "He shyly called in Lawrence Lewis to his aid, & trans-
fixed me with a Dart. I . . . was obliged to submit & bind myself
to become that old fashioned thing called a *Wife* & I am perfectly
reconciled neither think 'the day *evil*, or the Hour *unlucky.*'"
Although "submit" and "bind" and "reconciled" were unusual
words to express her enthusiasm for her impending marriage,
now that she had found someone who so perfectly fit her
requirements, Nelly Custis was in love. "The Man I have chosen
to watch over my future happiness, is in every respect calculated
to ensure it."

But Lawrence wanted to set up housekeeping on his property
in Frederick County, and the possibility of being separated from
the Washingtons and Mount Vernon worried Nelly as her wedding day approached. "For me, my prospects of happiness
although very great are yet clouded when I think of leaving My
Beloved Grandparents who have been everything to me hitherto,
& this dear spot — which has been my constant Home."

In 18th-century Virginia it was necessary for a fatherless bride
to choose a guardian in order to obtain a marriage license on her
behalf. Nelly, of course, chose her stepgrandfather. Washington
wrote to Lawrence of his errand to Alexandria on January 21,
1799, "wither I went to become the guardian of Nelly, thereby to
authorize a license for your nuptials on the 22nd of next month."
The wedding was set for Friday, February 22, Washington's 67th
birthday, obviously as a gesture of respect and affection for
Nelly's Grandpapa.

"An event occurred on the twenty-second of February, 1799,
that, while it created unusual bustle in the ancient halls, shed a
bright gleam of sunshine on the last days at Mount Vernon,"
wrote George Washington Parke Custis in his memoirs. On the
evening of what was to be Washington's last birthday, dear
friends and close relatives, including Nelly's mother and her sisters, gathered in the candlelit house overlooking the icy river and
watched George Washington give his Nelly away in marriage.
The Reverend Thomas Davis, Rector of Christ Church in
Alexandria, officiated. The bride wore "something white, beauti-

ful too." Washington wore his old Continental buff and blue, and a simple black cockade. Martha was dressed "in a light flowered satin." The Washingtons presented to the bridal couple an American silver tea service, bearing the monogram LEPL topped by an eagle with outstretched wings. Before retiring to bed, Washington wrote in his diary with his usual brevity, "Miss Custis was married ab^t Candle light to Mr. Law^e Lewis."

Some of the wedding guests remained at Mount Vernon for almost two weeks. After their departure, the newlyweds left on a round of visits to Lewis and Custis relatives. On her honeymoon, Nelly again mourned the separation from her grandmother, "I left my Beloved & revered GrandMama with sincere regret, & it was sometime before I could feel reconciled to traveling without her." Unbeknownst to Nelly, her grandmother was seriously ill during her absence. But Nelly was not informed because the Mount Vernon family knew she would have hastened back to pay her grandmother "every dutiful affectionate attention in my power." Lawrence was not well either, spending four weeks of his honeymoon in a darkened room in the home of his brother George Lewis with an inflammation in one eye.

While the newlyweds were at the home of Charles Carter, Lawrence's brother-in-law, Lawrence received a letter from George Washington dated September 20, 1799. "It has been understood from expressions occasionally dropped (from Nelly Custis, now) your Wife, that it is the wish of you both to settle in this neighborhood," his uncle wrote. Washington explained his intention to give his adjacent Dogue Run Farm to Lawrence on which to build a home. He planned to give "that part of my Mount Vernon tract which lies North and West of the public road

ON FEBRUARY 22, 1799, GEORGE WASHINGTON'S
LAST BIRTHDAY, NELLY CUSTIS MARRIED LAWRENCE LEWIS, SON OF
WASHINGTON'S SISTER BETTY LEWIS. ALTHOUGH FEW DETAILS
ARE KNOWN ABOUT THE CEREMONY, THIS 1899 ENGRAVING, AFTER
H.A. OGDEN, DEPICTS ONE ARTIST'S VERSION OF THE HAPPY EVENT.
WILLARD-BUDD COLLECTION,
MOUNT VERNON LADIES' ASSOCIATION.

leading from the Gum Spring and Colchester (from a certain point which I marked) containing about two thousand acres of land." Still aware of Lawrence's lack of self motivation, he was giving him, in addition to the land, "the Mill, and Distillery, on a just and equitable Rent . . . it being necessary, in my opinion, that a young man should have objects of employment." Washington ended with a final note of admonishment: "Idleness is disreputable under any circumstances; productive of no good, even when accompanied with vicious habits."

When the couple returned to Mount Vernon, Lawrence accepted Washington's offer. Nelly rejoiced in the idea that she would be near her grandparents and their home after all. Plans were laid to build the Lewises's home on Gray's Hill, the highest elevation on the Dogue Run Farm, three miles northwest of Mount Vernon. The new mansion would take several years to complete, and in the meantime the Lewises were encouraged to remain at Mount Vernon.

Shortly after she returned from her honeymoon, Nelly contracted influenza, from which she suffered for four weeks. During her recuperation she learned that she would have a baby in late fall. "The idea of being a Mother," she wrote, "of watching over & forming the mind of Our little infant is a source of delight which none but those in similar situations can experience. I have been busily engaged in providing little trappins for the sweet stranger . . . My Belov'd GrandMama has also been employ'd for some time for her little great grandchild." Nelly found it hard to believe that she "who was generally stiled a thoughtless giddy mortal extremely fond of going to Balls" had become a "sedate matron" attending to domestic duties and preparing for the birth of the child who would call her mother. Nelly's own mother came to stay with her during the final days of her pregnancy. On November 27, 1799, after the arrival of Dr. James Craik and a midwife, Nelly gave birth to a daughter, Frances Parke Lewis. The day would also have been the birthday of John Parke Custis, Nelly's father. Nelly laid her new baby in a walnut crib, a gift from her grandmother.

THE CRIB GIVEN TO NELLY CUSTIS LEWIS BY MARTHA
WASHINGTON WHEN NELLY'S FIRST CHILD WAS BORN STANDS
IN THE NELLY CUSTIS BEDROOM AT MOUNT VERNON.
FRANCES PARKE LEWIS WAS BORN AT MOUNT VERNON ON
NOVEMBER 27, 1799, LESS THAN THREE WEEKS BEFORE
GEORGE WASHINGTON DIED IN A NEARBY BEDROOM.
MOUNT VERNON LADIES' ASSOCIATION.

On December 9, Lawrence Lewis and George Washington
Parke Custis left Mount Vernon to conduct business in New Kent
County. Three days later George Washington came back from his
usual ride with snow on his collar and hair. The following morning he complained of a sore throat. Before retiring that night,
Tobias Lear suggested he take something for his throat. "No,"
Washington answered, "You know I never take anything for a
cold. Let it go as it came." Sometime after two in the morning he
awakened Martha to tell her he was ill, suffering from an acutely
sore throat and difficult breathing. Because the room was cold,
he would not allow his wife to get out of bed to call a servant. In

the morning Dr. Craik was sent for. And so, less than 20 days after the birth of Nelly's first child, Washington lay dying of quinsy in the room beyond hers. So soon after childbirth, Nelly was confined to her bed and could not go to see him. It would have required her to go down the main staircase and up the private, narrow stairs to her grandparents' room. George Washington died in the evening of December 14, 1799, without his Nelly beside him. But he died knowing that his careful plans for his granddaughter's future happiness were well on the way to fulfillment.

Washington's remains were laid out in the large dining room. Ten months after he had officiated at the happy occasion of Nelly's wedding, Reverend Thomas Davis was summoned for Washington's funeral, which was held on December 18. Martha was too grief-stricken to attend. In her place Eleanor Stuart served as the principal mourner. Lawrence Lewis and Nelly's brother were still away, and Nelly too was prevented from "paying the last sad duties" to her grandfather because of her confinement. Letters of condolence came by every post, and the task of answering the more intimate ones fell to Nelly. To a Philadelphia friend she wrote, "The loss we have sustained is irreparable."

As a woman of the 18th century, Martha Washington knew that death was not to be discussed, grief not to be shown. To contemplate death was to succumb to it. Having seen her husband's resignation to his approaching death enabled her to submit to her own. "All is now over," she said after he breathed his last. "I have no more trials to pass through. I shall soon follow him." She closed the bedchamber they had shared for nearly a quarter of a century and moved to the austere garret chamber, heated by an iron stove, on the mansion's third story, directly over Nelly's bedroom.

Perhaps the presence of Nelly's little Frances Parke eased Martha's inner pain and grief. Another child, Martha Betty, named after Nelly's grandmother and Lawrence's mother, was born to the Lewises in August 1801. By then Frances Parke had become her great-grandmother's pet. "Frances is the darling of her good GrandMama and seems to afford her comfort and amusement,"

Nelly wrote. "My Beloved Parent is delighted when my child is fond of her, calls her GrandMama and just gives her sweet kisses. My only fear is that my daughter will be spoilt, she is indulged in everything . . . she takes a fancy to." Nelly's fear of Martha's indulgence was reminiscent of her own mother's worries when Nelly and Martha became so closely attached. But Nelly found delight in seeing her venerable parent lavishing attention on her own child.

Nelly must have sensed that her life was changing. Her Grandpapa was gone, and her grandmother's health was failing. Her own health had been poor since her marriage. Now she was raising children of her own at Mount Vernon. But soon she would be forced to leave the home she loved for a new house of her own. With the turn of the century political changes were also evident. In 1800, the nation's capital was moved to the new Federal City, 16 miles north of Mount Vernon. That autumn, President John Adams moved into the new president's house, later called the White House, and Congress convened in the city for the first time. Thomas Jefferson, Washington's Antifederalist adversary, was elected the new president. Nelly agreed with her grandmother that Jefferson was "one of the most detestable of mankind," and his election was "the greatest misfortune the country has ever experienced." Nelly claimed her hatred of the man was a result of "the abuse he offered Washington while living, and to his memory since his decease." When Elizabeth Bordley wrote Nelly that she had heard that her friend had dined at the executive mansion with President Jefferson, Nelly quickly wrote back setting the record straight, "You are misinformed . . . I have not the honor to be in that great *man's graces*, nor can one who knew so well the *first President*, ever wish to be noticed by the present chief magistrate."

In December 1801, there was a family Christmas gathering at Mount Vernon, the last that the Custis and Stuart families would spend there. Nelly wrote, "My eldest sisters have been with us here since Christmas. My sister Law also dined with us on Christmas day."

After a visit to Mount Vernon in January 1802, William E. Curtis recorded his impressions of Washington's widow: "Mrs. Washington appears much older than when I saw her last in Philadelphia, but her countenance is very little wrinkled and remarkably fair for a person of her years. She conversed with great ease and familiarity, and appeared as much rejoiced at receiving our visit as if we had been her nearest connections." The reporter added, "We were all federalists which evidently gave her particular pleasure." By March, Martha looked "badly and had a wretched cold." She told a guest "that Life was no longer desirable." Nelly tried to make her grandmother as comfortable as possible in her garret chamber. She read to her from the Bible and sang hymns for her, and together they sewed or knitted.

On May 20, Thomas P. Cope visited Martha and made the following entry in his diary:

> The pleasure which we had anticipated in this visit was greatly diminished by the illness of Lady Washington. She is confined to her bed & from the account given by Doctor Craik, the family physician, has not many days to survive . . . . The death of her husband affected her sensibly. She had not entered either his study or the apartment in which he died since the removal of his corpse, nor can any entreaty induce her to change the lodging room which she selected under the roof & which is a small, inconvenient, uncomfortable apartment. She now promised Doctor Craik that should she recover from the present attack, she will consent to lodge in some other part of the house more airy & commodious; of this there is little probability as her health has been wasting for the last twelve months & yesterday a chilly fit deprived her, during the paroxym, of the power of speech. He thinks another must deprive her of life.

Two days later, Martha died. On the night of her grandmother's death Nelly's children were both suffering from the measles. Frances Parke survived, but Martha Betty died the following month. Nelly herself was confined to bed with a rash and a fever. She was also pregnant again. Her mother was called once more to do "the honors of the House and Table" at Martha's funeral. A mourner described Nelly as "the Picture of Woe. never did I see silent Grief so strongly marked as in her countenance. she did not shed a tear, and scarcely breathed a sigh — poor Soul. . . . I feel for her most sincerely, and fear she will sink, under the accumulated suffering, of Mind and Body. losses so rapid, and of so dear, require great exertion of Piety, and strength of Mind to support these qualities I am sure she possesses and now they will be called to action."

There was an interruption of five years in Nelly's letters to Elizabeth Bordley. For a time, her grief remained private. Undoubtedly the losses she had suffered were devastating, because now the separation from her grandparents was final.

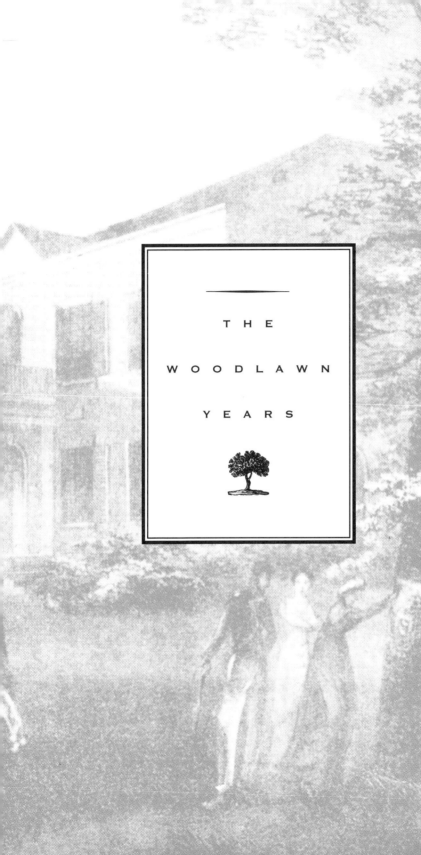

THE

WOODLAWN

YEARS

"A Variety of Changes"

*U*ntil the death of Martha Washington in 1802, Nelly and Lawrence Lewis had continued to make their home at Mount Vernon while construction was progressing on their new home, which was being raised on Gray's Hill, overlooking the Potomac River and Dogue Run, three miles inland from Mount Vernon. The mansion would be called Woodlawn after an ancestral home of the Lewises. Nelly had written to her friend Mrs. Pinckney that after the house was completed in a year or so and they had moved in, she hoped to be "well and comfortably fixed — then shall I expect my good friends will have some curiosity to see me a house-keeper, and if possible, allow me the delight of entertaining them as amongst my most wellcome Guests."

In accordance with George Washington's will, Mount Vernon was inherited after Martha Washington's death by Judge Bushrod Washington, Washington's nephew and the oldest son of Washington's favorite brother John Augustine. Bushrod Washington, who had served as his uncle's legal advisor, was a lawyer practicing in Richmond, Virginia when he was appointed to the Supreme Court by President John Adams in 1798. The judge and his wife Ann were anxious to occupy the house. George Washington Parke Custis offered to buy Mount Vernon, but the Washingtons were not interested in selling the home. So in 1802 Nelly, Lawrence and baby Parke were forced to move from Mount Vernon to Western View, the home of Betty Carter, Lawrence's older sister in Culpeper County. That autumn the Lewises moved into the north wing of Woodlawn, the only portion of their new house yet habitable.

In December of 1804, Nelly resumed her correspondence with her childhood friend Elizabeth Bordley. She wrote "that neither time or the variety of changes I have experienced, has diminish'd the sincere affection I have felt for you since our first acquaintance." Nelly's mention of the variety of changes that had occurred was an understatement. The familiar way of life Nelly Custis Lewis had known and loved had changed completely. During the five years her letters to her friend were interrupted, both of Nelly's grandparents died, she gave birth to four children, two of whom died, and she was pregnant again. She had suffered from almost constant ill health since her marriage. And she had moved from the security of Mount Vernon to an unfinished home of her own. The effect of these changes was Nelly's excuse for not having written sooner. She explained that "sickness and sorrow, are not very favorable to epistolary communications."

In her first letter to Elizabeth, Nelly mourned for the days when her grandparents had been the center of her life. "Ah my Beloved friend, how sadly times are changed to us all, but to me more than anyone, deprived of those Beloved Parents whom I loved with so much devotion, . . . I look back with sorrow, & to the future without hope — it appears to be a dream long passed away, so heavily has time passed to me." The death of Martha was the heaviest blow of all. Nelly lamented the loss of "her tenderness and unceasing care of me, & the reverse is so dreadful, that I shall never know happiness again." So, only five years after marriage and motherhood, and two years after becoming the mistress of her own home, Nelly, at the age of 25, looked to the future with little hope or happiness.

Designed by Dr. William Thornton, the first architect of the U.S. Capitol, Woodlawn was constructed of red brick in the Georgian style. The central block of two stories contained a par-

lor, music room, dining room and master bedroom on the first
floor and four bedrooms and a linen room on the second floor.
Wide halls connected the rooms upstairs and down. One-story
identical hyphens on the north and south ends of the house
joined the main house to the kitchen and library. The mansion
was spacious and comfortable, but it bore little resemblance to

THE LEWISES MOVED TO WOODLAWN PLANTATION
IN 1802, FOLLOWING THE DEATH OF MARTHA WASHINGTON,
BUT THE HOUSE WAS NOT FINISHED FOR SEVERAL MORE YEARS.
*COURTESY OF WOODLAWN PLANTATION, A PROPERTY OF THE
NATIONAL TRUST FOR HISTORIC PRESERVATION.*

Mount Vernon. Its exterior was much more like Kenmore,
Lawrence's family home in Fredericksburg.

Woodlawn's surrounding landscape lived up to its name. A cir-
cular drive led to the west front of the mansion, bordered by a
wilderness of oaks, magnolias, tulip poplars and hollies. Around
the estate were dogwoods, roses and flowering shrubs. Nelly her-

self tended the little gardens or flower knots that she planted around the mansion in honor of each of her children. Woodbine spread its flowering tendrils over the entire north wing of the house. To the south of the mansion there were fruit trees, a kitchen garden and a magnificent tall pine tree that the Lewis family nicknamed "General Washington."

Woodlawn's high elevation afforded a view of the red shingled roof of Nelly's former home. Although during George and Martha Washington's lifetime Nelly had considered it a great advantage to be so near Mount Vernon, now the proximity of Woodlawn to Mount Vernon seemed less a blessing. From her windows, Nelly looked upon the home that represented the happy life she no longer shared with her grandparents. "I live now in sight of Mount Vernon, and it is a continued source of uneasiness to reflect on times past which can never be recalled," she wrote. But memories of the Washingtons were not only beyond the windows. Woodlawn's rooms were largely furnished with Mount Vernon decorations. Martha had willed to her granddaughter looking glasses, tables and chairs, prints, china, silver and glassware. At Mount Vernon's estate sale held in July 1802, two months after Martha's death, the Lewises had purchased bedsteads, blankets, a "Moonlight painting" and even a chicken coop. In the music room, standing amidst other instruments, was the harpsichord her Grandpapa had given her.

After a Christmas visit with the Lewises at Woodlawn, Judge David Daggett wrote, "Their house, after the manner of that part of the country, is an elegant spacious mansion . . . . In that (to us) lovely place there is much to delight all who have a taste for the comforts and elegancies of life. The house and every article of furniture is in a style suited to the nephew and granddaughter of the most respectable George and Martha Washington."

Nelly encouraged her friends to visit Woodlawn, particularly Elizabeth Bordley. "It is not a Virginia fashion to pay *short* visits, & I shall be very averse to parting with you. — come then my dearest soon as possible, and permit me to do all in my power to make you happy in my House." Presidents, politicians and military officers came from Washington City for sleighing parties when the snow was deep. After dinner the guests were ushered into the music room, a very important place in the Lewis home. Nelly's love of music prevailed at Woodlawn. A visitor described the room as being "an elegant parlour, well stocked with musical instruments, harps, pianos, violins; masses of books lay on every table, and maps and elegant plates decorated the walls." A typical after-dinner serenade included music on the harpsichord and guitar by Nelly and her daughter Parke, who also sang and played the harp. Like his father, her son Lorenzo played the violin because "his chest will not bear the flute." But Nelly feared her son would "torment catgut and murder music a long time before he plays a tune decently."

Added to Woodlawn's guest list were Nelly's many relations, who often stayed for several weeks or months. Her sister Martha Peter came from her Georgetown home, Tudor Place, along with her daughters Columbia, America and Britannia. George Washington Parke Custis, who had built a home of his own, Arlington, overlooking the Potomac River and Washington City, came with his wife Mary. Their daughter, also named Mary, was one of Nelly's favorites. Her niece was still unattached, and Nelly thought that there were few suitors worthy of her. Mary Custis would later marry a young lieutenant named Robert E. Lee, and Nelly played the harpsichord at their wedding.

Nelly Custis Lewis's burden of responsibility in the rural south was far greater than was Elizabeth Bordley's in the crowded city of Philadelphia. The duties of a plantation mistress required skill, efficiency and careful management. Housewifery included overseeing five main areas of responsibility: feeding the family and guests; making the family's clothing and keeping it clean; keeping the home and making household essentials; serving as doctor and nurse for all the members of the family as well as servants and slaves; and caring for children, both her own and the children of relatives who may be staying with the family. Frugality and self-sufficiency ranked high among southern homemaking virtues. In an age when printed cookbooks were rare, one of Nelly's most important companions was her housekeeping book, a bound volume in which she wrote recipes, home remedies, laundering methods and household hints.

The numerous visitors to Woodlawn required careful management of food stores. Nelly complained to Elizabeth Bordley that as the mistress of a Virginia plantation she had to "give up music & painting, for pickling, preserving & *puddings.*" Nelly had to keep her smokehouse full of meat all year long, her root cellar and pantry had to be stocked and ready for the winter. During the summer her garden had to have an ample number of vegetables and herbs, and her fruit trees needed to be producing in their seasons.

Because of lack of refrigeration, much food was eaten that we today would have considered spoiled, and a housewife employed many methods to insure her food would last. Eggs, for instance, were preserved by covering them with paraffin. Slaughtering was usually done in the late fall after cool weather had arrived to prolong the life of the meat. Beef and pork were salted for preservation. Meat was buried in salt or was soaked in a brine made of saltwater. Oftentimes the addition of saltpeter helped the meat retain its red color.

Successive crops had to be planted in the garden and put up so produce was available all year long. Root plants, which could be stored for winter consumption, had a longer life than salad greens, which were enjoyed in season. After harvesting, potatoes, carrots, turnips, radishes and cabbages were stored in the root cellar. Corn, peas and a variety of beans were dried and stored in containers. Onions, cucumbers, asparagus, mushrooms and walnuts were often pickled and turned into relishes. Of the fruits served at Woodlawn, the peaches, plums and apples were dried, and smaller fruits such as strawberries and raspberries were put in bottles and sealed. Some fruits that could not be canned were made into jellies or candied.

Nelly oversaw the baking once a week in the kitchen's bake oven. Since the Lewises owned a mill, given to them by Washington, they always had plenty of fresh flour. Nelly's housekeeping book contained recipes for soft gingerbread, thin biscuits and muffin breads. Nelly also recorded the directions for making a "Love Cake," a "Courtship Cake," and a "Matrimony Cake." The latter was probably used for the weddings of Nelly's children, two of whom were married at Woodlawn. Unlike the light confectionery wedding cakes of today, Nelly's recipe was for a spice cake, which included "1 pint of dough, 1 cup of sugar, 1 cup of butter, 3 eggs, 1 tea spoon of pearl ash, with raisins & spices." Like her stepgrandfather, Nelly served ice cream at her home. Ice was brought from the Potomac River in the winter and stored in the ice house on the east lawn. The frozen dessert was a unique summer treat.

Dinner was an enormous meal, both at Mount Vernon and Woodlawn. Although the food was prepared by the cook — and during Nelly's tenure at Woodlawn, there were several, including a man — it was necessary for the mistress of the house to supply the menu, the recipes, and the ingredients as well as to oversee the cooking process and the serving. When guests were fed it was time for a plantation mistress to be judged as to whether or not she was a successful housewife. Hence, a large variety of food was served as attractively as possible. Dinners at Woodlawn were served at 4 o'clock in two courses. The first consisted of soups, meats and vegetables. Tomatoes, although still somewhat of a rarity in the United States, were often included in the menu because the Lewis family was especially fond of them. The second course, made up of a variety of desserts, was served after the first tablecloth had been removed, revealing another beneath. Beverages served during dinner consisted primarily of spirits, coffee and tea.

Congressman Thomas Hill Hubbard recorded ample proof that Nelly practiced the lessons she had learned from her Grandmama concerning setting a fine table for her guests. "The table was spread with double cloths," he wrote, "and the first course consisted of beef, mutton, oysters, soup, etc. The first cloth was removed with these viands, and the clean one below covered with pies, puddings, tarts, jellies, whips, floats, floating island, sweetmeats, etc. and after these we came to the plain mahogany table. Clean glasses were brought on and a lighter kind of wine and fruit, raisins and almonds." The floating island that Hubbard mentioned was a fashionable dessert made of colored egg whites that were floated on a sea of sweetened cream.

As the plantation's nurse and doctor, Nelly dealt with many domestic ailments such as colds, flu, stomachache and fevers. She took her medical responsibilities seriously. Her skills were learned by experience. At Woodlawn, illness plagued the Lewis family constantly. On one occasion Nelly complained that her whole family was afflicted, "before one was out of his room another confined . . . . If we live 'till next June I trust we shall quit the vile foggy south for some months, I never wish to see it from June to November again." Treatments prescribed were sometimes more dangerous than the disease. Bloodletting, blistering and violent purges were often recommended. For a sore throat Nelly advised gargling with cayenne pepper. For a nosebleed, sugar of vitriol (zinc sulfate) dissolved in water was absorbed in a rag and stuffed up the nose. Her husband's gout and the headaches of which she constantly complained were illnesses that required more inventive panaceas.

According to Nelly, her migraine headaches forced her dependence on Marshall's seidlitz powders, a mild cathartic. "I could not live without them," she wrote. When suffering from a "rheumatic, nervous & bilious headache" she took four seidlitz powders with a cup of coffee, bound her forehead and temples with popular leaves, which she covered with a silk handkerchief and then flannel. Her remedy, she said, "produces a violent perspiration & consequent relief."

For her special friends she often made up a pot of her lip salve based on her grandmother's recipe. She even sent pots of it across the ocean to Lafayette's family at La Grange in France. Nelly listed in her housekeeping book her creative home cures for everything from consumption to mad dog bite. She purchased most of the ingredients for her curatives at the pharmacy shop of Edward Stabler in Alexandria.

The large-scale production of cloth that had gone on at Mount Vernon was not repeated at Woodlawn. Nelly made most of her children's clothes, but she purchased the fabrics on trips north and then dyed them to the desired color herself. She considered the fabrics sold in Washington City and nearby Alexandria to be inferior. Colored dresses and flannel were laundered in warm milk. Common clothes such as muslin, silk and cambric were boiled in water with hard soap. Gum Arabic was used as a starch, and the clothes were ironed while still damp. Nelly continued to pass what little free time was available to her by doing fancy needlework. She made keepsakes for her children and friends and decorated her home with footstools, pillow covers and fire screens.

It was to Elizabeth Bordley that Nelly turned to purchase many goods that she could not manufacture herself or buy locally, because she considered the local products available to be sec-

PORTRAIT OF ELIZABETH BORDLEY GIBSON, NELLY CUSTIS'S
LIFELONG FRIEND AND CORRESPONDENT, ATTRIBUTED TO ANDREW WALLACE
AFTER GILBERT STUART, *CIRCA* 1820.
*COURTESY OF WOODLAWN PLANTATION, A PROPERTY OF THE NATIONAL TRUST
FOR HISTORIC PRESERVATION.*

ond-rate. Until the time when the Lewises experienced some financial reverses, almost every letter she wrote included some request for Elizabeth to procure something from Philadelphia for her friend in Virginia. "I hope you will pardon the trouble I give you," she wrote, "but I prefer everything from Phia in preference to the works of the district — because they understand, & execute, matters of taste, far better, in your City." Nelly requested everything from corset laces and harp strings to mattresses and dimity curtains. Oftentimes there were requests for art supplies such as paint or brushes. There were also requests for objects that would be used to complete Nelly's needlework pieces such as screen handles, purse clasps or frames.

Naturally this ordering of articles by mail was a very slow process, a lesson George Washington had learned when he ordered wares from England. This was particularly true in regards to Nelly's request for shoes. Nelly asked Elizabeth to have six pairs made for her at Kraft's on Walnut Street. A month or two later the handmade shoes arrived at Woodlawn. Sounding rather exasperated Nelly wrote back, "They are all too large . . . . I am very sorry to give you so much trouble, my Dear Friend, but you know shoes stretch so much that if too large at first, they are soon very uncomfortable." The shoes were packaged up and given to the servant whose job it was to ride to the post office in Alexandria every morning. Six months later, Nelly finally had a few pairs of shoes that fit correctly.

One of the most unusual items Elizabeth was asked to procure was requested by Nelly's daughter Parke. "Father wishes to have a wig — his hair has fallen off since his illness, and his head will require it — at present he wears a silk cap lined with flannel. I take the liberty of enclosing the size of his head to you." She asked that it be made "of grey — hair, like the lock which accompanies the pattern." The wig also took several return trips to Philadelphia before it was made to fit Lawrence properly.

Nelly always accompanied her requests with the entreaty to put her goods "into the inside of the stage[coach], if possible, as they will be less liable to injury than they would be behind."

Elizabeth never refused any of Nelly's requests and never mur-
mured a word of complaint in supplying her faithful friend with
those things she needed on her Virginia plantation.

Just as a planter's success was measured by his crops and
income, a plantation mistress was judged by her household management. And at Woodlawn, Nelly displayed proof not only that
her Grandmama was a good teacher, but also that Nelly had
learned her lessons well in regards to household industry. She
had discovered that the home was virtually the only place a superior woman could distinguish herself.

"Amour Maternelle"

Although Nelly's role as Woodlawn's mistress required a great deal of initiative and executive ability, it was not the role she considered her most important. It was her role as a mother to which she was most dedicated. Nelly gave birth to eight children, four of whom lived past infancy. The loss of her grandparents and four of her children in less than 13 years, as well as the suffering from the death of her own mother in 1811 and the suicide of her former tutor Tobias Lear in 1816, were blows from which Nelly never fully recovered. The remainder of her life would be devoted to her surviving children. Elizabeth Bordley wrote of Nelly, "Her motto, 'Amour Maternelle' was fully sustained & acted upon — no losses or sorrow could ever weaken it — when children died, she transferred it to grandchildren, and with uniform strength of mind, she sustained all trials and clung to remaining duties."

Frances Parke Lewis was Nelly and Lawrence's first child. Born on November 27, 1799 at Mount Vernon, "Parke," as she was called, had been her great-grandmother's pet. August 19, 1801 was the birthday of Martha Betty, who died of the measles at the age of 10 months shortly after the death of Nelly's Grandmama. Coming so close after the passing of George and Martha Washington, Nelly wrote after the death of her second daughter that Martha Betty had been "released from a sorrowful world." Lawrence Fielding, named for his father and his grandfather, was born August 5, 1802 at Western View, the Lewises' temporary home. He died immediately after his birth. Lorenzo, born on November 13, 1803, was the first child to be born at Woodlawn, and he would be the Lewises' only son to survive past childhood. Eleanor Agnes Freire was born at Woodlawn on August 8, 1805. Fielding Augustine was born two years later on July 2, 1807. He lived to the age of one year and seven months. Born on February 14, 1810, George Washington Custis lived for only one year and nine months. Mary Eliza Angela was born on April 1, 1813 and was her parents' youngest child.

Nelly wrote, "Life has no charm for me unless when emply'd in the care of my children." Parents of the 19th century were distinguished by their insistence that their children were their only comfort in life, their sole source of happiness, their only reason for being. Although this was certainly the case in Nelly's feelings concerning her relationship with her children, there were a variety of circumstances that helped to make Nelly a mother representative of her time. Certainly as a result of the loss of her children, Nelly cherished even more those children who survived. But Nelly's devotion to her children also followed the pattern set by her grandmother. And she earnestly tried to avoid the errors made by her own mother and her sister.

Nelly considered her grandmother a model of womanhood. And certainly it was Martha's pattern of child rearing that Nelly most often followed. Until Patsy Custis's early death, Martha's daughter was seldom far from her mother's sight and influence. Nelly was also constantly under the scrutiny of her grandmother. It was traditional for the mother or, in Nelly's case, her grandmother, to oversee all areas of her daughter's life. Nelly's grandfather oversaw her education, and he stepped in to give her advice on courtship and marriage. But, as evidenced by Nelly's letters, Lawrence suffered from chronic bad health and had little initiative in regards to the rearing of children. As a result, Nelly became the major influence in these areas of child raising as well.

ONE OF THE MOST BEAUTIFUL PORTRAITS OF NELLY CUSTIS AS A YOUNG
WOMAN IS GILBERT STUART'S "MRS. LAWRENCE LEWIS," *CIRCA* 1805.
NATIONAL GALLERY OF ART, WASHINGTON. GIFT OF H.H. WALKER LEWIS
IN MEMORY OF HIS PARENTS, MR. AND MRS. EDWIN A.S. LEWIS.

Nelly had learned by a mistake made by her own mother. Eleanor Stuart had given up her daughter at a young age, and as a result, her conscience was troubled for a long time afterwards. Like her mother, Nelly suffered from much ill health at the time of the birth of her children, but she never considered sending her children out to be raised. The close emotional relationship a mother quickly developed with her infant undoubtedly stemmed, at least in part, from late 18th- and early 19th-century mothers' commitment to nursing their own babies. Nelly said she knew "no delight equal to nursing." Mothers who were forced by illness to send their babies to wet nurses were considered unfortunate, as in the case of Eleanor Custis when Nelly was born. The close relationship Nelly sought to develop with her children was one she never had with her own mother.

Nelly was also influenced by the unfortunate circumstances surrounding the marriage and separation of her oldest sister Eliza. After her marriage, Eliza remained the headstrong, impulsive person she had been in her youth. Eccentricities also emerged in the personality of her husband, Thomas Law, who was twice his wife's age. The Laws lived in a beautiful house on Capitol Hill where they gave splendid parties, but their conflicting personalities soon collided. In 1802, Law went to England looking for real estate investors and did not return for two years. When he returned to Washington in 1804, the couple were divorced. The reason Nelly gave for their separation was a "difference of dispositions." Eliza's stipulated yearly income from Law, $15,000, was erratic and so were her emotions and style of living. Her volatile marriage had produced one daughter, also named Eliza. Nelly wrote that she opposed her sister's separation and had "endeavour'd to reconcile them for their childs sake." After her daughter married and had three children, Eliza accused her son-in-law Lloyd Rogers of moving his family too far out of their grandmother's reach. Eliza, who was now calling herself Mrs. Custis, became resentful of her sister Martha Peter's security and luxurious home and what appeared to be Nelly's enviable life at Woodlawn. She was estranged from all of her family, but what grieved Nelly the most was the end of Eliza's relationship with her own daughter. In 1832, Eliza died without any of her family at her bedside.

It was natural for Nelly to regret Eliza's estrangement from her daughter most of all. As they grew older, sons followed in the footsteps of their father, but daughters remained in the sphere of their mothers. A mother concentrated her attention on her daughters. Living in a world dominated by men, mothers and daughters turned to each other for support and companionship. Nelly's firstborn, Frances Parke, and her mother enjoyed a typical 19th-century mother/daughter relationship — one of friendship and affinity.

When Parke was seven, Nelly was teaching her daughter to read, and although Parke was progressing rapidly, Nelly admitted, "I believe I am not well calculated for an instructress." But Nelly had to do her best. Living so far from the city made it impossible to procure day teachers. By the age of 11, Parke was playing very well on her mother's harpsichord and on the harp. Nelly brought out many of the early musical pieces she herself had trained on. Her mother wrote that Parke also had "an excellent talent for drawing." She longed to take Parke to Philadelphia where she would be afforded the same benefits of education that her mother was fortunate to have had. But Nelly complained that Virginia farmers were too busy to leave their homes. She continued to lament her own inadequacies as an instructor for Parke. As a plantation mistress, whose time was so often spent overseeing a diverse household, Nelly claimed to have forgotten much of her own stock of knowledge, "Indeed [I] am becoming a very humdrum character." Although Nelly's situation proved that a city education was not necessary for a woman destined to spend her life on an isolated plantation, she still wanted that education for her daughter.

By the fall of 1814, Nelly put aside her own regrets at losing her daughter's companionship when she took Parke to Philadelphia to enroll her in the school of Madame Greland. On this trip, Nelly was reunited with Elizabeth Bordley in whose hands she put the care of her 15-year-old daughter. After Nelly returned home she wrote to Elizabeth, "It was indeed a severe trial to part with my darling Daughter who was my companion & friend, but to comply with her ernest wish, & to benefit her, as I trust it will in every respect, I could submit to any sacrifice. — I cannot suppress my anxiety about her."

Caring for her other children, Agnes, Lorenzo and little Angela, took up much of Nelly's time, but it was obvious from her correspondence that her thoughts were often in Philadelphia with Parke. Nelly's letters to Elizabeth were filled with concerns about Parke's health, safety, manners, accomplishments, etc. She asked Elizabeth to guard "*our* daughter" against the shoals and quicksands that Parke would encounter in the perilous voyage of life. She insisted that Parke continue to practice her music, just as Martha had made Nelly practice daily on the harpsichord. She asked her friend to learn how Parke conducted herself in large company, and she was curious about the general opinion of Parke's deportment. "Excuse the anxiety of a Mother who is much more ambitious for her Daughter than she ever was for herself." Nelly claimed to have written volumes of letters of advice to Parke, but she appealed to Elizabeth to give Parke practical illustrations that would be more impressive. "And when My Beloved Child is with you, instill into her mind those feelings of right which may guard her when removed from your protecting care." Nelly was grateful to learn that all of her old friends from the years of her grandfather's presidency in Philadelphia had embraced her daughter as well.

When Nelly heard a report of typhus fever spreading over the households of Philadelphia she became distraught. She begged Elizabeth for news. Was her child safe? Was she dressed properly against the March winds and April showers? She instructed that Parke must not go where there was even the smallest risk of contracting the disease. With so much distance separating them there was little that Nelly could do but commit her daughter to the care of the Almighty. The reports of widespread disease turned out to be only a rumor.

In the summer of 1815, Parke returned to Woodlawn for a brief vacation from her schoolwork. Although Nelly loathed the thought of sending her daughter back to Philadelphia, she valued Parke's "happiness too much, to deprive her of the advantages she must derive from a residence with Madame G." Parke would not return right away, however. "Mr Lewis was seized with the gout in his foot," Nelly wrote, " . . . and not being willing that I should enjoy a pleasure which he had mark'd for himself, she must of necessity wait until the gout releases him." In the meantime Nelly heard another false report that yellow fever prevailed in Philadelphia. Although Nelly was primarily concerned about Parke's safety, she was also worried for her "valuable Friends whom it would grieve me much to suppose in danger." This time Elizabeth had a doctor write a note to Nelly calming her fears and stating that once again the report she had heard was a false one.

After Parke returned to school, Nelly was "mortified" to receive a report that her daughter's posture was not as good as it should be. She stooped too often! Her concerned mother had a collar and backboard made for Parke that was just like the brace Nelly had worn as a young girl in hopes of conquering the "dreadful habit." In addition, she requested Elizabeth "remind her, whenever she is with you, of this defect, and admonish her to correct it." In the fall of 1817, much to Nelly's relief, Parke returned home from school in good health, with improved manners, and a fine education. Like her mother, Parke was a woman of many accomplishments. She was fluent in Latin and French, and she was a talented artist and skilled musician.

In June of 1820, the Lewises visited New York, and then traveled on to Philadelphia where they stayed with Elizabeth and her new husband, attorney James Gibson. There they enrolled their 14-year-old daughter Agnes in the school of Madame Greland, the same school attended by her older sister. Nelly considered Madame Greland to be unequaled as an instructor for young women. At Woodlawn that summer, Lawrence suffered a variety of illnesses, including dysentery and gout. Nelly served as her husband's nurse and still managed to be able to keep up the frantic correspondence she had carried on with Elizabeth while Parke was attending school. In October of 1820, Nelly's worst fears were realized when Agnes became critically ill. The doctors were having no success in treating her, and her mother was summoned to Philadelphia. For almost two weeks Nelly sat by her daughter's bedside. "I cannot give up nursing her myself I should suffer more from anxiety than fatigue." Elizabeth answered Nelly's requests for the ingredients for a variety of remedies with which Nelly attempted to bring down Agnes's dangerously high "bilious fever," as well as to soothe her stomach pains and violent coughing. Nelly's vigil ended with Agnes's death on October 28.

Nelly wrote to Parke, "Your Angel sister went off like an infant asleep. I stood by her the whole time." After writing her daughter's obituary for the Philadelphia newspaper, Nelly wrote that she was perfectly composed, but she added that she could not live through the same trial again. Two days later she wrote, "They say my Child has not changed yet, if so I cannot have her put into her coffin unless certain proofs of her being past recovery appear." Nelly's concern was not unlike George Washington's, who had asked on his deathbed that his body not "be put into the Vault in less than three days after I am dead." When Nelly was assured that her daughter was past recovery, 15-year-old Eleanor Agnes Lewis was laid to rest in the churchyard at Christ Church in Philadelphia where her mother had worshiped as a young girl during Washington's presidency.

"She is ever before me, in health & in her last illness, but I do not wish to forget her ever," Nelly wrote after her return to Woodlawn. She asked Elizabeth to go to the churchyard and notice how Agnes's grave was covered. Earlier in the summer she had given silhouettes of Agnes to Elizabeth and a number of friends, now she found she only had one left and none for her children. She asked Elizabeth to go to Charles Willson Peale's museum and have a dozen more cut. But when the profiles arrived at Woodlawn, Nelly could not bear to look at them.

Nelly held Madame Greland responsible for her daughter's death. She vowed to never again let one of her children live under her care. "I regret most bitterly that my child was far from me when timely & proper attention & medical advice might per-

haps have saved her — & is not Madme G the cause of that."
Nelly's grief was not a silent one like her grandmother's of the
past century. Nelly expressed her sorrow in her letters to
Elizabeth and by writing verses. And at Woodlawn she planted
a memorial to her dead daughter, using all of Agnes's favorite
flowers. Nelly often visited the grove where she had carved her
daughter's name in the trunk of a tree. One of her poetic compositions ended:

> To the spot thou most loved do I repair,
> And with kisses embalm thy Dear Name,
> To meet thee in Heaven is ever my prayer,
> And my last sign shall murmur the same —

Nelly no longer wore anything but black, and she admitted
that she had not danced for 22 years. Now, nothing could ever
move her to do so again. She had lost all taste for what had once
been an amusement that she had enjoyed above all others.

The following year the cloud of Agnes's death still hung over
Nelly. In search of peace of mind, she turned to her clergyman.
"We had a long conversation at night & most soothing & delightful it was to hear him speak of my blessed Angel." As in the 18th
century, ministers were more likely to counsel the female members of their congregation rather than the males. Religion
remained necessary for women, but was dispensable for men.
Religion gave women a certain independence from their hus-
bands. In Nelly's case it was God in whom she placed her confi-
dence, and it was Him to whom she turned in times of need.
Women of the 19th century turned to a religion that was more
sentimental and more evangelical than their ancestors had
known. But the chief message of religion to women and men
was the same — resignation to God's will. Women believed that
the Lord loved those whom he chastened, and Nelly interpreted
the death of her children as proof of God's love. She believed
that peace would come only when she accepted her family's suffering as God's will. Resignation to the death of a beloved child,

however, was a difficult lesson for a devoted and loving mother to learn. Still, Nelly found solace in the belief that her dead children were now in a better world. In the next two-and-a-half years Nelly would suffer from the death of more close relations. "In less than thirty months, eight of my nearest connexions have died," she wrote in 1822. A decline in Nelly's once bubbly good spirits was all too evident in her letters.

In 1821, Lorenzo Lewis, at the age of 18, left Woodlawn for Yale College in New Haven, Connecticut. Nelly again agonized over the trial of parting from another of her children. She knew that a city education was best and having to send "Lolen" away was part of "the misfortune of living on a Virga Farm"; however, she claimed it cost more in parting with her children than it was worth. By spring of 1823, Lorenzo had completed his studies and had returned home. In an effort to detach her son "from the idle life which he necessarily leads here & in Alexa," Nelly wrote to Elizabeth asking if Lorenzo could study law under her husband, James Gibson. "Mr. L & I are very anxious to give our dear son some useful employment . . . . We think that Mr. G's example & advice as to Law, & reading, & morals, & conduct, will be of lasting advantage." Nelly requested that Elizabeth find Lorenzo a room near her with a carpet and fire at which to board. But when Lorenzo arrived in Philadelphia he demonstrated his ability to take care of himself by finding a room of his own, ignoring the recommendation of Mrs. Gibson. This was one of the few examples that any of the Lewis children might have resented their mother's interference. In spring of 1824, it must have felt to Nelly as if Agnes's deathbed scene was to be repeated when she received word that Lorenzo was suffering from delirium and convulsions. Once again Nelly hastily traveled to Philadelphia to nurse her child. This time the danger passed. Lorenzo recuperated.

The year after she sent Lorenzo off to Yale, Nelly began to consider the education of Angela, her youngest. As she had with Parke and Lorenzo, Nelly found that teaching Angela at home was not easy: "I am doing all in my power for her myself, — but, interrupted continually by domestic duties, company &c, is necessarily too much neglected, & has not steadiness enough to go on well unless I am near her." Nelly would not consider sending her away to boarding school by herself after what happened to Agnes. Although Nelly wanted Angela to have every advantage, she refused to be separated from her. In fact, Angela even slept with her mother. "She sleeps in my bosom always," Nelly wrote to Elizabeth in 1825. With Parke's help, Nelly did the best she could teaching her daughter, and Angela too learned to play on her mother's harpsichord. In the meantime, Nelly tried to convince Lawrence to let her and Angela travel to Philadelphia where their daughter could attend day school. Nelly planned to take her to school in the morning, call for her in the evening, and continue to sleep with her at night. She wrote to Elizabeth that if Lawrence came to visit, he could have a bed in the parlor. Nelly longed to move her family away from the isolation of rural Virginia to the city of Philadelphia. "Oh for a house in Chestnut Street, that we might study the graces, the arts & sciences, one & *all of us*." Philadelphia was not just the happy location of the scenes of Nelly's youth, but it was the place where she wanted to return in order to give her family the best educational and social opportunities, not only for them, but for herself as well. But Lawrence claimed that he could not afford to send his wife and daughter to Philadelphia. A disappointed Nelly, who seldom had the opportunity to leave the grounds of Woodlawn, complained that "I am almost a vegetable."

In January 1825, Nelly welcomed visitors to Woodlawn who took her mind off her burdensome household affairs and family demands. The Marquis de Lafayette, who was almost 70 years old and the last surviving general of the Revolutionary War, returned to America "to see for himself, the fruit borne on the tree of liberty." His visit coincided with the 50th anniversary of American independence. Besides touring the entire east coast, the Frenchman and his son, George Washington Lafayette, planned to visit Woodlawn, Mount Vernon and Arlington. These two men stirred in Nelly scenes of her childhood when the Marquis first visited Mount Vernon, and later years when his son had sought refuge with the Washington family. Nelly had the same feelings for the Marquis that she had for her grandfather, with equal affection for his son whom she considered a brother. She so looked forward to the day when she would see the "one who almost idolized the Gen'l and Grandmama, & the friend & Brother of my happy days." When Lafayette and his son arrived at Woodlawn they were warmly greeted by the Lewises and their children. Nelly was overjoyed to have the devoted friend of her grandparents under her roof. Once again crowds of well-wishers came to pay their respects to the aging hero. One smug Virginian reportedly observed that the Marquis's manners were notable for their great simplicity. "They must have been formed by the elevated behavior of the Virginia gentlemen with whom he associated during the Revolutionary War."

THE LITHOGRAPH "WOODLAWN, SEAT OF LAWRENCE LEWIS NEAR MOUNT VERNON," WAS MADE BY JOHN ROBERT MURRAY IN 1825, WHEN LAFAYETTE MADE HIS TRIUMPHAL RETURN VISIT TO AMERICA. LAFAYETTE CAN BE SEEN IN THE CENTER FOREGROUND WITH LAWRENCE LEWIS. GEORGE WASHINGTON LAFAYETTE, FRANCES PARKE LEWIS AND NELLY CUSTIS LEWIS ARE ON THE RIGHT. THE PRINT IS THE EARLIEST KNOWN VIEW OF WOODLAWN. *COURTESY OF WOODLAWN PLANTATION, A PROPERTY OF THE NATIONAL TRUST FOR HISTORIC PRESERVATION.*

While Lafayette continued on his tour, George Lafayette remained in Washington. Nelly went to stay at her sister Martha Peter's house, Tudor Place in Georgetown, to be near him. This must have been a very happy time for Nelly because she spent much time with this man who was the same age as she and with whom she had once been linked romantically by the press. Together they attended a White House drawing room. This was Nelly's second visit to the president's house during the administration of James Monroe. In 1822 she had written to Elizabeth, "I went to a drawing room, the first I have been at since The Genl was President — I had few acquaintants, & really felt *alone in the crowd*. The *royal family* were as attentive & gracious as I could have desired."

This visit to the White House was during President Monroe's last full month in office. In the fall of 1824 John Quincy Adams had defeated General Andrew Jackson in the race for the presidency. General Jackson was a personal friend who always referred to her as "Dear Nelly," and she regretted his loss bitterly. "The papers will tell you of our disappointments," Nelly wrote Elizabeth, "& I hope also, that we have more cause to be proud of Andrew Jackson defeated, than the Adams party have of their *Clay* Prest. . . . I shall not visit Mrs Adams at all — I do not respect her husband & I despise his Father."

While he was in America, George Lafayette's mother-in-law died in France, and it was Nelly who consoled him. "Poor George is most painfully situated as he cannot leave his Father, & is so far from a wife whom he adores — He has the best heart in the world — He comes every day to us, & I much prefer exerting myself to console him as far as possible for *friendship* to accomplish, to any party that I could attend." George Lafayette gave Nelly an engraving of his father, which was hung in an honored place at Woodlawn. She presented him with a brooch she had specially made in Philadelphia, with Elizabeth Gibson's help, that contained locks of George and Martha Washington's hair.

The elder Lafayette returned to Woodlawn in early spring. The day before their departure, the Marquis showed to Nelly a picture of his wife that he wore around his neck, and permitted her to kiss it. It was a favor that his own children had enjoyed only once. George said to Nelly, "I am happy to think that you have received from my Father, the most tender proof of affection in his power to bestow." On the Mount Vernon wharf she embraced them both before they boarded the steamboat. Lafayette returned to his native France with a trunk full of American soil that he wanted spread over his grave.

Nelly described the visit of the Marquis to Elizabeth, "We have had the happiness to receive him here . . . . He was very happy here & paternally affecte. I love him most devotedly. I felt as if my own great adopted Father was in my house . . . . It was a feast for me while I staid, & I was weeping for three days after he left us." Months later Nelly still recalled the visit fondly, noting that "It appears now like a pleasant dream, that they have been here." With great sorrow she wrote, "I never anticipate the happiness of being with them again, in this world."

Although Nelly still had not found a tutor to come to Woodlawn and teach Angela, Lafayette had left in his wake a "Spanish Patriot," Seqor Conasco, who tutored Nelly in the Spanish language. "I am in raptures with it & resolved to persevere until I am a good Spanish scholar . . . but Mr. L . . . cares for no language but English, & thinks it nonsense for me to learn; but it is certainly an innocent gratification, & I will learn myself." Nelly turned to her friend for the encouragement her husband would not give her, promising to show Elizabeth all of her translations. Nelly was amused at herself for becoming a scholar again at the age of 47. When Angela began music instruction in Alexandria, which meant that Nelly and her daughter had to spend three nights a week in town, Nelly complained about the interruption of her Spanish lessons.

In 1823, Nelly had written, "There is a perfect rage for marrying this year, I think, I never take up the papers that I do not see several announced." Nelly was undoubtedly disturbed by the fact that Parke's wedding was not one of those included. At the age of 24, with not a serious proposal, Parke was an old maid by the standards of the day. Nelly was satisfied with having her daughter as her constant companion, but she was concerned that if Parke did not find a husband before her mother's death, Nelly did not know who would sustain her daughter through that trial. One thing was sure, Nelly did not want her daughter to marry a Virginian, not even a Southerner because "I know too well, the evils attending the *slave* property, not to wish that my children may never encounter them." Like George Washington, Nelly supported gradual emancipation.

There was another disadvantage to living in the South. Having spent years trying to have her children properly educated, Nelly realized that in the South education was very little attended to. In order to have their children educated, Southern parents had to send their children away to school.

Elizabeth Gibson agreed with Nelly's concerns and thought that Parke's lack of marriageable prospects put her in a "state of *safety*." "May she continue free from the spell," Elizabeth added. Nevertheless, she suggested that Nelly find some eminent beau who might be induced to move northward. Nelly and Elizabeth were anxiously plotting to get Parke involved in what her mother called the "marriage lottery."

In a letter reminiscent of the one Washington had sent to Nelly concerning the selection of a mate, Nelly advised Parke that there were more important qualities when choosing a suitor than riches or social standing. Wealth or pageantry of greatness were not important. Nelly knew this because in the persons of her adopted parents she had seen "what real greatness consists in." Nelly advised her daughter to consider "mind, manners, & every recommendation most desirable in a matrimonial connexion." Speaking from her own experience, she also advised her daughter against marrying an older man. Parke assured Elizabeth that when she made a choice, her fiance would "strike all beholders with admiration."

A long list of eligible suitors came to Woodlawn and stayed for supper and a Lewis family musicale, which on one occasion lasted until 1:30 a.m. But Parke had become "indifferent to all sons of Adam." As time went by and Parke was still not engaged, her mother convinced herself that no one was good enough for Parke, and that Parke was better off remaining single. In a gossipy letter to Elizabeth, Nelly described one particular admirer, a senator from Louisiana, as "a monkey" who she felt was not good enough for her daughter. Nelly even went so far as to tell the suitor's friends to discourage his attentions to Parke.

Another suitor, a "Major Cooper," more closely fit Nelly's requirements for a suitable mate for her daughter. But she considered the fact that he was a widower a serious liability — an interesting opinion, Nelly herself having married a widower. As each beau came and went, Parke's wedding seemed more and more an "uncertain event."

Then Lieutenant Edward George Washington Butler came to call at Woodlawn. "He has been much in the world," Nelly wrote to her friend, fulfilling her promise that she would write Elizabeth immediately after a genuine suitor was accepted by Parke. "[He] is a favorite wherever he is seen & known, & possesses, without exception, the most guileless heart & temper I have ever known in one of his sex. — a very affecte & grateful heart." Lieutenant Butler came from a distinguished family. He was the son of Edward and Isabella Fowler Butler. His father had been a Revolutionary War hero, and at the elder Butler's death, which occurred at Fort Lebanon, Tennessee, while in military service, young Edward was placed under the guardianship of General Andrew Jackson. He was graduated from West Point Military Academy. Named after Nelly's grandfather, Butler was also born on February 22.

By spring of 1825, Parke and Butler were engaged. "He is the choice of my dear Child, after mature deliberation she says . . . . She is willing to be a Soldiers wife, to follow his fortunes . . . . She is convinced she says that this roving life will make her happy." Nelly wasn't so sure. After having heard about her grandmother following General Washington to winter camp every year during the Revolution, she doubted that Parke would be satisfied to take "up her tatters & follow the drum."

THE MUSIC ROOM AT WOODLAWN TODAY FEATURES TWO
PERIOD HARPS TO REPRESENT THE INSTRUMENTS PLAYED BY
NELLY CUSTIS'S DAUGHTER PARKE, AND AN EARLY PIANO
SIGNIFYING NELLY'S ACCOMPLISHMENTS AT THE KEYBOARD.
*COURTESY OF WOODLAWN PLANTATION, A PROPERTY OF THE
NATIONAL TRUST FOR HISTORIC PRESERVATION.*

As her daughter's wedding day approached, Nelly began to
have serious doubts about Butler being a suitable match for her
daughter. She described Butler's character and disposition as
"unexceptionable" and "inferior." She complained that he was not
of "such a *mind*" as she thought Parke would have selected.
Nelly wrote that she trembled at the thought of the difficulties
and the privations her daughter would have to endure as the wife
of a soldier. And if Butler was stationed far away and Parke
became pregnant, Nelly thought her daughter was too weak to
endure the ordeal without her mother nearby.

Parke was married on April 8, 1826, a "merry wedding"
according to her mother. Afterward the newlyweds left for their
frontier post in Cincinnati, Ohio, where Butler was stationed
under General Edmund Pendleton Gaines. For the next year

Parke enjoyed far better health than she had ever experienced under her mother's care, and she was expecting a baby in February. Nelly longed to be with her daughter, but she did not want to leave Angela. When Nelly came down with the mumps in December, the possibility of being with Parke during her confinement was eliminated. Nelly's concern was a legitimate one. Statistics proved that during childbirth the chances were high that either the mother or the baby would not survive the ordeal. According to Nelly, the baby boy was born two months premature but was "fat & healthy." The mother was fine and Nelly rejoiced in being a grandmother. Parke dedicated her baby to "God & Country," and the six-day-old baby "*smiled* his determination to redeem the Pledge." Nine months later the baby died.

In February of 1828, without ever having told her mother that she was pregnant, Parke gave birth to stillborn twin girls that she had carried for only three months. Shortly afterwards, Colonel Butler was transferred to New York, and Parke returned to live temporarily at Woodlawn, where on June 4, 1829, she gave birth to a healthy baby boy who was named after his father. Nelly announced the news to Elizabeth and added, in what must have seemed to her friend like a very ironic statement, "My poor Parke . . . is so anxious & dotingly fond of her little darling that I fear she will make herself always miserable about him."

While Lorenzo was living in Philadelphia, working under James Gibson, he had become engaged to Esther Maria Coxe, whose father Dr. John Redmond Coxe had served his apprenticeship under the prominent physician Dr. Benjamin Rush during the tragic yellow fever epidemic of 1793. Esther's mother was a childhood friend of Nelly's. In regard to her son's bride, Nelly wrote, "I rejoice that I can without hesitation, adopt his choice as my Beloved daughter." Lorenzo brought Esther home in the summer of 1827. The couple planned to reside at Woodlawn while Lorenzo developed his own plantation, Audley, outside Berryville, Virginia, in Clarke County. Nelly turned many of her housekeeping duties over to her new daughter-in-law, of whom she was very fond. On February

12, 1829, Esther gave birth to a son. He was named George
Washington Lewis.

In January of 1833, Elizabeth Bordley Gibson invited Angela to
visit her in Philadelphia. At the age of 19, Angela had never been
parted from her mother for any extended length of time. Nelly,
who would have liked to have visited Philadelphia as well, wrote
back to Elizabeth reminding her friend that "we always share the
same bed." But Angela went alone because Lawrence was ill
again and Nelly had to remain home with him. Angela's arrival in
Philadelphia was followed by a note to Elizabeth from her mother, "I trust you will not permit *her head to be turned* in your
delightful city." While Angela was away Nelly had a nightmare in
which she dreamed she was dying and was unable to see her
daughter a last time. But Nelly's fears of being separated from her
youngest child were ended when Angela returned home in
March. Nelly wrote to Elizabeth saying that her friend was fortunate in never having become a mother because she would never
have to suffer the anxiety caused by raising children.

When General Gaines considered relocating back west, Nelly
worried that long distances would again separate her from her
daughter Parke. Nelly claimed she would give anything if Butler
was independent of the army. It was so inconvenient to depend
on the "caprice of these generals." In 1833, Butler resigned from
the army and moved his family to Dunboyne Plantation in
Iberville Parish, Louisiana, where he had purchased a sugar
cane plantation.

In November, the Lewises left on a three-week journey to
Parke's new home. Nelly found her daughter's house small,
"indeed only a cottage." But she was fascinated by the unusual
scenery, particularly the view from River Road, which passed in
front of the gate to Parke's plantation and bordered the
Mississippi River from New Orleans to Natchez. Nelly thought the
immense oaks and magnolias around the plantation were splendid. And when the planters burned off their sugar cane tops all
along the banks of the river, it was a beautiful and brilliant night-
time spectacle. But Nelly found the pendulous gray moss that

hung from the trees gloomy, a feeling that she thought echoed her daughter's situation. This was exactly the life she did not want for her daughter. Parke's days were spent in "domestic toil." Choctaw and Natchez Indians came to the house trading handmade baskets for food. There were no schools or churches for many miles. "Sunday among the French & Creoles . . . is like any other day," Nelly lamented.

For the next several years Nelly, Lawrence and Angela spent their winters with Parke. Every year they learned of Butler's failure to bring in a good crop. In 1835 a destructive freeze killed the orange and lemon trees and a great part of the sugar cane. What remained of his harvest was lost on its way to Richmond. Butler had to plant cotton to supplement his meager income. Nelly continued to complain about Parke's situation. Perhaps it was too much like her own in rural Virginia. Parke was "literally buried alive, her health her spirits destroy'd by over exertion, no congenial mind or pursuits to compensate for domestic drudgery."

The Lewis family's extended visits to Louisiana gave Angela an opportunity to socialize with friends of her own age. According to her mother, Angela was quite a belle and at one time had three acknowledged captives in her train. One in particular was her "perfect shadow" and devoted himself so entirely to her that at last he gained victory. In the spring of 1834, Angela became engaged to Charles Magill Conrad, a 27-year-old lawyer from New Orleans. Nelly wrote that she never saw any young man so universally beloved and respected as he was by all the classes in the state. Although she had wanted no one from the South as a mate for her youngest daughter, Conrad, who was a Virginian by birth, won her heart. Nelly wrote that he would have been her choice had she the whole world to select from. "Indeed he is all I have ever known or heard of, the best calculated to make us all happy in my darling's choice." Angela and Charles Conrad were married at Woodlawn in the summer of 1835. They settled in Pass Christian, Mississippi, on the shores of the Gulf of Mexico.

Nelly rejoiced in her daughter Angela's match but she continued to hope for better for Parke. Of the seven children Parke bore, four lived to maturity. Parke instructed her children in Latin, French and English as well as in musical accomplishments. Besides making the better part of their clothing, she made all of her own. Nelly continually pressed her daughter to visit Woodlawn, but Parke felt she could not leave her husband while they suffered from severe debt as a result of unsuccessful planting.

With both of her daughters settled in the South, Nelly and Lawrence considered moving to Louisiana. It would be painful to part with Lorenzo and his family, but Nelly thought her place was with her daughters. "Mr L intends to buy a small place near our Parke, and if he lives, to remove our negroes this fall & try to make cotton," Nelly reported in 1835. "That climate suits him best, & it is best to be near our darling children." But the move never occurred. While Nelly resided with her daughters, Lawrence stayed at Audley, Lorenzo's home.

In 1837, Angela gave birth to a son who was named after his father. Two years later she had another boy, Lawrence Lewis Conrad. The delivery was difficult and Angela never fully regained her health. When Nelly first heard of her daughter's illness, Lawrence, as the last surviving executor of George Washington's estate, was overseeing an addition to the new tomb at Mount Vernon. Nelly delayed her departure for Mississippi. By the time the new tomb was completed and Nelly arrived to nurse her daughter, it was too late. Angela had died at the age of 26 on September 21, 1839, of what her mother termed "congestion of the brain." With sorrow, Nelly wrote, "Of eight children I have outlived six — but to all but this last beloved & most excellent child, I have been permitted, by the Almighty, to pay the last duties, to resign them myself into the hands of Him who giveth & taketh away — & that was a consolation in my bereavement." Nelly returned to Woodlawn with her two infant grandsons. Mary Eliza Angela Conrad was later buried just outside of the new tomb at Mount Vernon.

CHAPTER SIX

"Exiled"

"Woodlawn is worse than nothing," Lawrence Lewis wrote to his son-in-law, referring to the farmland given to him by George Washington. Worse than nothing because it required an enormous amount of time and energy, as well as money, but produced very little. Lawrence had learned the same lesson Washington had learned years before at his Mount Vernon farms. As a result of a century of tobacco planting, Virginia's soil was badly depleted of necessary nutrients. Like Washington, most Virginia planters had converted to other crops that did not deplete the land's fertility. Wheat, corn, and other grains were planted in rotation where once only tobacco had grown. But the growing of cereal was hardly the stuff of grand fortunes. Although farther south large plantations continued to thrive as a result of cotton, sugar cane and rice, tobacco was largely responsible for the end of the great plantation society in Virginia. Many planters suffered from symptoms of mental anguish as they let acres go fallow or sold them to small farmers.

To add to the woes of Virginia planters, in 1819 a severe depression rocked the country, and agriculture prices began an appalling downward spiral. Virginia was particularly hard hit. The depression continued throughout the 1820s. Land values, exports and slave prices all fell. The depression required that planters put a great deal more effort and steadiness into their planting than most aristocratic Virginians were inclined to supply.

Lawrence Lewis was never an accomplished or innovative planter. He planted because he had been given land by George Washington, not because he had any real inclination for the raising of crops. A short military career and work as Washington's secretary did not adequately prepare him for the role of manag-

ing almost 2,000 acres of farmland. Naturally, poor land halfheart-
edly farmed would produce a meager harvest. However,
Woodlawn was not unlike other Virginia plantations, which were
also experiencing economic difficulties at this time. Lawrence's
farm in Frederick County was also failing. "Our Farm here never
very productive is worse than ever," Nelly wrote. "This has been
a dreadful winter to us — The wheat appears to be entirely
destroyed here & in Fredk our stock suffers very much & no
grass yet to sustain them, corn to buy & negroes to feed who
make nothing, this is a gloomy prospect, is it not?"

Certainly, Lawrence's chronic ill health did not help his success
as a farmer any more than it helped his marriage. Lawrence was
continually afflicted by his weak eyes. Gout in his legs caused
him pain throughout his life. Occasional trips to bathe in natural
warm springs were only a temporary remedy. By 1821, "flying
gout" required that Lawrence take an opium pill every night. On
one occasion, Nelly wrote that her husband suffered from "gout
in the head," the contemporary term for manic depression, and
resulted in a severe case of vertigo. A planter who was periodi-
cally confined to his bedroom, unable to attend his affairs, could
hardly be prosperous.

Nelly had written that George Washington had never
refused her anything. There was no doubt that she had been
spoiled by the life she had led in Philadelphia and at Mount
Vernon. During the first years at Woodlawn, the Lewises main-
tained a similar lifestyle of high social standing, but when
Lawrence's health began to deteriorate, Nelly suddenly found
herself without many comforts. This inevitably led her to com-
pare her husband to George Washington, a formidable proto-
type against which to measure anyone. Lawrence blamed Nelly
for managing household finances unwisely. He regarded the
income from Woodlawn and his other farms as adequate but
judged his wife as being too extravagant. He wrote that Angela
often mentioned "the subject to her mother, & always under
the mildest persuasion, but alas the habit had become a disease without a cure."

PAIR OF PORTRAITS OF LAWRENCE AND ELEANOR PARKE
LEWIS, ATTRIBUTED TO JOHN BEALE BORDLEY, 1832.
*PHOTOS BY EDWARD BARR, COURTESY OF WOODLAWN
PLANTATION, A PROPERTY OF THE NATIONAL TRUST FOR
HISTORIC PRESERVATION.*

To Elizabeth Gibson, who made several visits to Woodlawn,
Nelly appeared the dutiful wife. "Her husband, Major Lawrence
Lewis, was an invalid & retired early every evening to his room,"
Elizabeth wrote, "and no matter what engaged her with company
in the parlor, she invariably left us for awhile to comfort him by
reading a Bible chapter & singing a hymn." But Nelly was not
entirely sympathetic. She criticized her husband, who was 12
years her senior, for being a weak man and a financial failure.
And she wrote with the same realization that had caused George
Washington to turn the Dogue Run Farm and the mill over to him
in the first place, "Mr L is not the most energetic of men."

In the 19th century, a wife was supposed to exist for her husband, be an agreeable and obedient companion to him, a tender
mother of his children, a capable and industrious manager of his
house, and a gracious and attractive hostess to his guests. In
reading the voluminous correspondence from Nelly to Elizabeth,
it is obvious that Nelly's life did not revolve around her husband.

There is a noticeable lack of mention of Lawrence in Nelly's correspondence. His name appears only when she blamed him for
their financial predicament, or when Nelly impatiently wrote of
his latest illnesses. On occasion, when Lawrence was well
enough to travel, Nelly complained to Elizabeth that her husband
was taking a trip but refused to take her along, saying he could
not afford the extra expense. After Lawrence made a trip to
Philadelphia Nelly wrote, "I owe him a *grudge* for not taking my
Daughters & myself on this pleasant & health giving journey —
we were all anxious to go." In 1821, Lawrence wanted to take
Parke along on a trip to Saratoga. But Nelly refused to let her
daughter go. Her excuse that she could not be parted from her
children selfishly denied them the enjoyment of traveling as well.

After both of her daughters had married and moved to homes
of their own farther south, and Lorenzo had moved over the
mountains to Audley, Woodlawn became a lonely and isolated
place for Nelly. She had once written that she preferred the quiet
of the country to city gaieties. Now it was too late to change her
mind. Woodlawn never had the attraction to visitors that Mount
Vernon had. Most travelers who made the pilgrimage to the home
of George Washington bypassed the home of his stepgranddaughter. As the years passed, Nelly missed the engaging conversation
and the coming and going of cultured guests, although the
Lewises could never have afforded the expense of entertaining the
crowds of callers that had burdened Mount Vernon. At Woodlawn
she felt "exiled" from the "society I love so much."

Nelly's sorrows compelled her to remember the old times.
"I often wish that I could go back again, & live over a few of my
early years — They were the golden age of our Country, as well
as ours." With each passing year she turned further to the memory of her grandfather, whose heroic image grew larger and larger.
She busied herself distributing countless mementoes of George
Washington's to fill the many requests. She cut out sentences and
signatures from his letters, saving only a few of the most personal
for herself and her children. Using the skill of the needle learned
from her grandmother, she fashioned a pin cushion and sent it to

a friend, describing it as "an old relick of past happy times." It was made of silver tissue that was a part of Martha's wedding petticoat when she married Washington. The lining was a part of the dress her Grandmama wore to the last birthnight ball in Philadelphia. Nelly sent Elizabeth a bookmark she had made, picturing flowers and a Bible, explaining that it was worked from special floss which her revered Grandmother had wound and given to her 57 years before.

When her brother, George Washington Parke Custis, asked her to supply him with details for a biography he was writing on George Washington, she relished the opportunity to reminisce about her relationship with the general in order to stop some of the "abominable falsehoods" being printed about him. Custis, who had dedicated himself to memorializing his stepgrandfather and had turned his home Arlington into a veritable museum of Washington relics, asked his sister to describe the visit of Jean Antoine Houdon in October of 1785 to Mount Vernon. The French sculptor had come to America to make a plaster bust of Washington on which to model a full length statue commissioned by the commonwealth of Virginia. Nelly wrote to her brother,

> I was only six years old at that time, and perhaps should not have retained any recollections of Houdon & his visit, had I not seen the General as I supposed, dead, & laid out on a large table covered with a sheet. I was passing the white servants Hall & saw as I thought the corpse of one I considered my Father, I went in, & found the General extended on his back on a large table, a sheet over him, except his face, on which Houdon was engaged in putting on plaster to form the cast. Quills were in the nostrills. I was very much alarmed until I was told that it was a bust, a likeness of the General, & would not injure him. This is all I recollect . . . .

As Nelly grew older she complained of a number of illnesses besides her migraine headaches. A "diseased liver" caused pains in her side and occasionally left her incapacitated. A visit to her daughters resulted in a serious back injury, the effects of which she would suffer for many years. Her steamboat had landed early in the morning after a great deal of rain. While descending from the upper deck of the boat, her foot slipped. She fell from the upper to the lower deck, striking her back against every step as she went down.

As a result of her feelings of isolation and her confining illnesses, Nelly relied on her correspondence with Elizabeth Bordley Gibson even more. Elizabeth was not only a link to the past, but she was also a link to the social and cultural activity of Philadelphia, a place where Nelly still longed to live even though she chastised the city in her letters for never having raised a monument to honor George Washington. It is not surprising that, given Nelly's unfulfilling marriage and her feelings of isolation at Woodlawn, the bond between her and Elizabeth grew stronger. "I crept into your heart slyly," she wrote Elizabeth, "when you were very young, and not so prudent as you now are, and having once gained possession, I would not suffer you or *any one else* to dislodge me."

One important event in Nelly's life went unmentioned in her letters to Elizabeth. Unlike the profusion of grief Nelly expressed in her letters after the deaths of her children, no mention is made about her feelings upon the death of her husband in any of her surviving letters to Elizabeth Bordley Gibson. On his way home from a visit to Audley, Lawrence Lewis caught a severe cold, forcing a stopover at Arlington, the home of Nelly's brother George Washington Parke Custis. He died there at the age of 72 on November 20, 1839.

The year after Lawrence's death Nelly went to Dunboyne Plantation in Louisiana to be with her daughter Parke and her grandchildren. Shortly after her arrival, Nelly learned that her son-in-law had told Parke that "he moved to La. to get as far from me as possible & he would be *damned* if he ever went where I was again, that my name was mentioned with ridicule & contempt throughout La. & even his poor wife suffer'd from it being known that I was her Mother — That I made my Husband miserable & shorten'd his days." Nelly argued that before her husband's death

Butler had begged them to pass the winters in Louisiana, and he had tried to persuade Lawrence to settle near him. In a letter explaining Butler's outburst, Nelly wrote that she thought that Butler had married Parke for her money, and now that her father was dead and she received no inheritance, Butler had unmasked his utmost contempt for his mother-in-law.

Parke told Nelly that she had concealed from her mother Butler's "outrageous conduct." Since their marriage, a pattern of violent behavior had emerged in her husband. Parke had suffered as a result of "ten years of sorrow & privations of every kind" and six years of "brutal treatment." Parke's children were so cruelly treated that Nelly's grandson, Loren, had told his mother that "he felt tempted to throw himself into the river & nothing but love for her prevented him." Nelly tried to give Parke her $1,000 annuity in order to get her daughter to leave Butler and return to Virginia, but Parke refused. Because of "the power he has over her poor children," Parke felt she would be leaving her five children to certain destruction. While Nelly packed her belongings to leave, Butler told her he was glad to see her go and hoped she would never return. He cursed Nelly and Parke, and "said he cared neither for her feelings or mine . . . I told him that I prefer'd his censure to his praise that I felt such unutterable contempt for him, I should dislike myself if he liked me." Nelly left her daughter's house feeling like an exile without a "friend, protector, or servant."

To her mother's relief, Parke's situation gradually improved as a result of newcomers to Iberville Parish, Louisiana. Reverend Fay, an Episcopal clergyman, and his wife, the daughter of the Episcopal Bishop of Vermont, moved to the area and opened a school and church two miles from Parke's home. Mrs. Fay, who had formerly directed a school in Savannah, took in 10 female pupils who boarded with her during the week and returned to their homes on weekends. Parke's children were taught all of the "good, useful, & elegant requirements." The Fays developed a close relationship with Parke and her children, and Nelly was glad that "after so many years without religious service, they have church now & communion service." However, Nelly's feelings about Butler remained unchanged. "I candidly confess that to hear he was dead will be a relief to me."

When Nelly returned to Virginia in May of 1841, she went to live at Audley, the home of her son and daughter-in-law. Many of Woodlawn's furnishings, including her harpsichord, were sent to Arlington, her brother's house, for safekeeping. Woodlawn, standing amidst fields of weeds, its garden paths no longer discernible and its rooms devoid of any cheer, was closed up. Down on the banks of the Potomac, Mount Vernon was also showing signs of deterioration and neglect. Judge Bushrod Washington and his wife had died in 1829. The estate was left to Bushrod's nephew John Augustine Washington. Upon his death in 1832, his wife Jane took over management until her son John Augustine Washington, Jr., came of age. But the subsequent owners of George Washington's estate had failed to stop Mount Vernon's decline as a result of financial difficulties, scavengers and time.

AUDLEY:

THE LAST

YEARS

"She Lived to Be Admired"

Audley was nestled in the quiet, meandering valley of the beautiful Shenandoah River under the shadow of the Blue Ridge Mountains in Clarke County, Virginia. The unpretentious house was low and sprawling with a large front porch. Although far more isolated than Woodlawn, Nelly never complained that she felt lonely at Audley. Besides Lorenzo and Esther, there were five of their six sons. Their oldest, George Washington Lewis, was attending school at the Virginia Military Institute in Lexington, Virginia. When Charles Conrad went to Europe in the summer of 1841, he left his two sons, Charles, Jr., and Lawrence, at Audley as well. Nelly wrote to Elizabeth, who as a result of deafness in one ear was using a hearing tube, "If you had our *seven* Boys in your house, all trying which could make the *most noise*, you would hear too much *without your tube* for your comfort." Being surrounded by her family revived Nelly's spirits.

In the fall of 1846, Parke returned to Virginia for the first time in 14 years. Accompanied by her youngest child, Lawrence, she came to place her two daughters, Eleanor and Caroline, in Miss Mercer's Seminary near Leesburg, Virginia, 25 miles from Audley. Parke's eldest son, Edward, Jr., was attending law school at Carolina College in Columbia, South Carolina. But Parke's visit to her mother was cut short because she needed to return to

Louisiana. A war was brewing with Mexico over the annexation of Texas, and Butler was expecting an appointment into the army from President James K. Polk. Butler hoped to be commissioned as a Brigadier Commander under General Zachary Taylor and was "chok full of fight but received no call." Nelly had written to Elizabeth during the summer, "You will be sorry to hear that Robt Lee, my nieces Husband, is ordered to Mexico — They have seven children — Mary and her family will remain at Arlington."

In 1846, 47 years after George Washington gave Woodlawn's acreage to his favorite stepgranddaughter and his nephew as a wedding gift, Lorenzo put the mansion and land up for sale. Woodlawn was sold for $25,000, considerably less than what Nelly thought it would bring. The home had never fulfilled the needs of his beloved Nelly as Washington had intended. Nor did it ever replace Mount Vernon in Nelly's heart. She said it was at Mount Vernon, not Woodlawn, where "the happiest years of my life were passed." Woodlawn was purchased by Quakers from Philadelphia who planned to cut down and sell Woodlawn's great trees for cordwood and ships' timbers.

Nelly's only surviving son, Lorenzo Lewis, died at the age of 57 at Audley in 1847 after two weeks of illness. Nelly prepared her son's body for burial, as she had done for her six other children who had preceded him in death. Esther took over the management of the estate and handled the affairs of Audley "extremely well" according to her mother-in-law.

In 1848, President James Polk laid the cornerstone for the Washington Monument in Washington City, but this did not improve his image in Nelly's mind. Polk was succeeded by General Zachary Taylor, who was greatly admired by Nelly because he was actuated by the same noble principles and had the same devoted patriotism that had distinguished George Washington, "& he will walk in *his* steps." Nelly always had a weakness in her heart for generals turned politicians, as in the case of her grandfather, Andrew Jackson and Zachary Taylor. At the age of 70, Nelly spent two weeks with the 12th president and the first lady at the White House, the residence of every president but George Washington. "Poor Mrs. Taylor is seldom quite well," Nelly wrote, "and the dirt and grease left by those detestable Polks is enough to make her sick. It is very strange that they did not clean up the house before the President and his family occupied it." After the president's house was put in order, Nelly sat with Mrs. Taylor upstairs in the private family quarters doing canvas work. In the evenings she entertained the president's guests by playing tunes she had learned in her youth, and she recounted stories of her grandfather in the first executive mansions in New York and Philadelphia. Nelly's days at the White House recalled the evenings when she was called upon by the first president to entertain his friends.

After only 16 months in office, President Taylor died in July of 1850. An unfinished letter to Nelly was found amongst his papers in which he described his journey to Richmond to lay the first stone at the base of the equestrian figure of Washington built on Virginia's Capitol Square. Nelly wrote to Elizabeth that his hope was "to go at no distant day to visit Mt Vn & Woodlawn with some one who has known those places & their owners in our palmy days, & could describe all to him." Nelly was especially pleased by the fact that Taylor told her she resembled his mother.

Shortly after the death of Zachary Taylor, Nelly suffered a severe stroke. She lost the use of her left side. For several months her face was drawn so that she could scarcely speak. She could not comb her hair, cut up her food or get into a carriage. The pain she suffered in lying down made her "dread the night." But she could still write to her old friend. "I felt convinced that I ought to feel *grateful* to God for his mercy in sparing my *mind* & my *right hand* — I felt that great as was my trial I had often *deserved greater*, & that it might have been far worse."

With the help of "Moreheads Galvanic machine, the flesh brush & divers medicines," Nelly's condition improved slightly and she was able to make one last visit to Woodlawn. Her former home was almost unrecognizable. "All the trees, the hedge, the flower knot, my precious Agnes's Grove, the tall pine Washington, *all gone*, in front a few trees & vines, but sweet recollections 'linger there still.'" When she returned to Audley, she wrote that she feared she would never cross over the mountain again. If Nelly had visited her beloved Mount Vernon, she would have seen the sad effects of time there as well. She never knew that in just a few years, Ann Pamela Cunningham and a group of patriotic women known as the Mount Vernon Ladies' Association would buy Mount Vernon from John Augustine Washington, Jr., and would begin their efforts to restore the home of Washington to its former glory. Nelly's harpsichord would be the first relic to be returned to Mount Vernon.

Now confined to a rolling chair, Nelly wrote, "This beautiful autumn I cannot participate in. I cannot go out of the house or in a carriage, I stand at the door, & seeing the green wheat, the beautiful mountains, inhale the sweet air, but my limbs are weak & I despair now of ever recovering entirely." When Elizabeth wrote asking how her friend spent her time, Nelly responded that she lived in her room except at mealtimes. She seldom went outside. She worked at her sewing until candlelight, and then read as long as she could keep her eyes open. She always rose before the sun and read her prayer book and Bible until breakfast was ready. Nelly planned to use her remaining years making needlework pieces for all of her grandchildren. So in her final days, Nelly was left with the two things that were firmly instilled in her by her grandmother, needlework and religious devotion.

In 1851 she learned of the death of George Washington Lafayette, her "faithful friend & brother." But she seemed to be especially moved when she heard of the passing of Andrew Allen, a friend from her days as a young girl in Philadelphia. "I recall him to my mind *now* when only 18 — how handsome how healthy, how witty & how agreeable he was, more so than any one I ever knew." Andrew had given her a beautiful ode on her 15th birthday, and although she had committed it to the flames before her marriage and never copied it, she could still repeat it perfectly. "I certainly should have loved him," she wrote. She asked Elizabeth to write her all she knew of him. Did he have children? What were his pursuits? And how did he use the brilliant talents he possessed? Did Elizabeth have a likeness of him late in life? "Do tell me if he ever spoke of me at all, & what he said."

Shortly before her death, Nelly reflected on her long friendship with Elizabeth Bordley Gibson. "Did I not with *my whole heart return* that faithful devoted friendship," she wrote, "altho' I never had opportunities to *prove* it by *acts* of kindness as *you,* my dearest Elizabeth had, yet it has never been less devoted than your own, & my gratitude will be as glowing, as imperishable as my affection. May I never mourn your loss, dearest friend." She was granted this last request.

Nelly Custis Lewis died on July 15, 1852, at the age of 74. It was a long journey from Audley over the mountains back to Mount Vernon. The hearse that brought Nelly home was followed by a single carriage in which rode two of her grandsons. Mount Vernon was reached late at night, and Nelly's remains were placed in the room where 53 years before she had gone forth a bride. Nelly was reunited with her grandparents again. The obelisk over her grave tells that she was the "Granddaughter of Mrs, & adopted daughter of General Washington," and was "reared under the roof of the Father of his Country, this lady was not more remarkable for the beauty of her person, than for the superiority of her mind. She lived to be admired . . . ."

MOUNT VERNON

By Eleanor Parke Lewis

As Lately I view'd Thee, dear Home of my Youth,
Those sweet shades I so fondly admired.
When bless'd with kind friends of tried honor & truth,
I possessed all my heart e'er desired;

I thought of years past, wing'd with joys ever new,
When I fear'd not afflictions keen dart;
When Parental affection so firm & so true,
Ev'ry bliss known on earth could impart.

Those halcyon days now forever are fled,
Yet while mem'ry and life I retain,
Still must I delight those lov'd paths to retread,
and, in fancy, lost treasure regain.

Those walks rever'd Washington, plan'd first by thee;
and the Tomb where thy ashes repose;
The shrine of my pilgrimage ever shall be,
'Tis a debt each American owes.

And of those who oft visit that much hallow'd spot,
Which thy virtues must ever endear;
Not a Son of the East how e'er humble his lot,
Ever shed there a crocodile tear.*

No the tears with which gratitude moisten'd that earth,
First caused thy tall cedars to wave;
And they still will be nourish'd whilst feeling & worth,
Shall inhabit the heart of the brave.

And although, in this world, we can never more meet,
Those whom, living, we lov'd and admired;
Let our hopes point to more blissful retreat,
That last Home by all Christians desired.

There were Angels, and glorified spirits above,
May we dwell in the "mansions of Heaven;"
Raise our voices in praise of our Savior Christ's love,
And to all, may salvation be given.

*Jefferson when Prest. U.S. a visit to Mount Vernon, and pretend-
ed to weep over the Tomb of Washington; Mr. Griswold, a distinguish'd member of Congress from —, gave soon after a publick
dinner, the following toast — "May the Tomb of Washington
never be profaned by Crocodile tears."

Copy of poem and Nelly Custis's footnote in the Mount Vernon Ladies'
Association collection; original in Farmington Museum, Connecticut, gift of Mrs.
Wilmarth S. Lewis, 1955.

CHRONOLOGY

1774	February 3, Jacky Custis marries Eleanor Calvert
1775	Custis child born and dies
1776	August 21, Eliza Parke Custis born
1777	December 31, Martha Parke Custis born
1779	March 31, Eleanor "Nelly" Parke Custis born
1780	Custis twins born and die
1781	April 30, George Washington Parke Custis born
	September 9, George Washington stops at Mount Vernon enroute to Yorktown
	November 5, Jacky Custis dies
1783	December 24, George Washington arrives home after Revolution
	Late, Eleanor Calvert Custis marries David Stuart
1789	April 14, Charles Thomson informs Washington of his election
	April 16, George Washington leaves Mount Vernon
	April 30, George Washington inaugurated president in New York
	May, Martha Washington, Nelly Custis and George Washington Parke Custis leave Mount Vernon
	May 28, Martha Washington and the grand-children arrive in New York
1790	Family moves to larger presidential house in New York
	September, family moves to Philadelphia
1791	Nelly Custis meets Elizabeth Bordley

1793	March 4, second inauguration in Philadelphia attended by all Custis grandchildren
	Summer and fall, yellow fever epidemic, 5,000 die in Philadelphia
	December, George Washington gives Nelly Custis new harpsichord
1794	March 9, Eliza Parke Custis and Martha Parke Custis visit for five weeks
	Summer and fall, Whiskey Rebellion in western Pennsylvania
1795	January, Martha Parke Custis marries Thomas Peter
	January, Nelly Custis receives letter from George Washington advising her on love
	March 31, Nelly Custis turns 17 and now wants to be called Eleanor
1796	Spring, Nelly Custis stays with mother at Hope Park
	March, Eliza Parke Custis marries Thomas Law
	April, George Washington Lafayette joins family at Mount Vernon
1797	March 4, John Adams inaugurated, Washingtons leave Philadelphia
	Fall, Lawrence Lewis arrives at Mount Vernon
1799	February 22, Nelly Custis marries Lawrence Lewis at Mount Vernon
	Summer, the newlyweds return from honeymoon and Nelly suffers from influenza for four weeks
	November 27, Frances Parke Lewis born
	December 14, George Washington dies
1800	Fall, Thomas Jefferson elected president
1801	August 19, Martha Betty Lewis born

1802	January 3, Eleanor Stuart has last child
	May, Nelly Custis Lewis and two children suffer from measles
	May 22, Martha Washington dies
	June 19, Martha Betty Lewis dies
	August 5, Lawrence Fielding Lewis born and dies
	Late summer, move to Woodlawn
1803	November 13, Lorenzo Lewis born
1804	Eliza and Thomas Law separate after eight years of marriage
1805	August 8, Eleanor Agnes Freire Lewis born
1807	July 2, Fielding Augustine Lewis born
1809	March 27, Fielding Augustine Lewis dies
1810	February 14, George Washington Custis Lewis born
1811	September 28, Eleanor Stuart dies
	December 16, George Washington Custis Lewis dies
1813	April 1, Mary Eliza Angela Lewis born
1817	Spring, Elizabeth Bordley marries James Gibson
1820	October 28, at age 15, Eleanor Agnes Lewis dies in Philadelphia
1824	Fall, John Quincy Adams elected president over Andrew Jackson
	December 11, Lafayette visits Woodlawn, Mount Vernon and Arlington
1825	January and February, Nelly Custis Lewis sees George Washington Lafayette often in Washington D.C.
1826	April 4, Frances Parke Lewis marries Edward George Washington Butler at Woodlawn, moves to Cincinnati
	December, George Washington Butler born in Cincinnati
1827	June 6, Lorenzo Lewis marries Esther Maria Coxe at Woodlawn

1828	Fall, Andrew Jackson elected president
1832	January, Eliza Parke Custis Law dies
1833	January, Angela Lewis visits Philadelphia without her mother
	December, Nelly Custis Lewis and Angela Lewis visit Frances Parke Lewis Butler in Louisiana for 8 months
1834	May, Lafayette dies
1835	July 30, Mary Eliza Angela Lewis marries Charles Magill Conrad at Woodlawn
1836	Summer-December, Nelly Custis Lewis with Frances Parke Lewis Butler at Iberville parish
1837	January-summer, Nelly Custis Lewis with Mary Eliza Angela Lewis Conrad at Pass Christian, Mississippi
1839	September 21, Mary Eliza Angela Lewis Conrad dies
	November 20, Lawrence Lewis dies (age 72), Nelly Custis Lewis (age 60) moves to Audley
1840	December, Nelly Custis Lewis evicted from Frances Parke Lewis Butler's home after fight with Edward George Washington Butler
1847	August 27, Lorenzo Lewis dies
1848	Fall, Zachary Taylor elected president
1849	April, Nelly Custis Lewis visits the White House for two weeks
1850	July 9, Zachary Taylor dies
	July, Nelly Custis Lewis suffers from a stroke
1851	Nelly Custis Lewis visits Woodlawn for the last time
	George Washington Lafayette dies
1852	July 15, Nelly Custis Lewis dies
1854	July 13, Martha Parke Custis Peter dies
1857	October 10, George Washington Parke Custis dies
1875	June 30, Frances Parke Lewis Butler dies

LEWIS FAMILY

Eleanor Parke Custis Lewis 1779-1852

m. February 22, 1799

Lawrence Lewis 1767-1839

1. Frances Parke 1799-1875

2. Martha Betty 1801-1802 (died age 10 months)

3. Lawrence Fielding 1802-1802 (died shortly after birth)

4. Lorenzo 1803-1847

5. Eleanor Agnes Freire 1805-1820

6. Fielding Augustine 1807-1809 (died age 20 months)

7. George Washington Custis 1810-1811 (died age 22 months)

8. Mary Eliza Angela 1813-1839

NOTES

Abbreviations Used in This Section

NC — Eleanor ("Nelly") Parke Custis Lewis

EB — Elizabeth Bordley Gibson

GW — George Washington

MW — Martha Washington

MVLA — From the collection of the Mount Vernon Ladies' Association

Writings — Washington, *The Writings of George Washington.*

The Mount Vernon Years

Page 3   "I have the pleasure to inform you": John Parke Custis to Martha Washington, October 12, 1781. MVLA.

Page 4   "on the eve of Christmas entered these doors": GW to Lafayette, February 1, 1784. *Writings,* vol. 27, p. 317.

"Mrs. Custis has never suggested in any of her letters": GW to Lund Washington, September 20, 1783. *Writings,* vol. 27, p. 157.

"He had just returned from Europe": Eliza Custis to David Baille Warden, April 20, 1808. MVLA.

"Two years after my father's departure": Ibid.

Page 5   "This sudden and unexpected blow": GW to Burwell Bassett, June 20, 1773. *Writings,* vol. 3, p. 138.

Page 6   "At any time I hope it is unnecessary for me to say": GW to John Parke Custis, June 19, 1775. *Writings,* vol. 3, p. 295.

"But what cou'd I do? . . . being a failure": Eleanor Custis Stuart to Tobias Lear, April 18, 1790. MVLA.

Page 8   "in a puny state": GW to William Gordon, November 3, 1784. *Writings,* vol. 27, p. 491.

"The little folks enjoy perfect health": Bourne, *First Family,* p. 101.

"under the shadow of my own Vine and Fig-tree": GW to Lafayette, February 1, 1784. *Writings,* vol. 27, p. 371.

Page 9   "There is no rest for me till I go to Mount Vernon": Lafayette to GW, August 10, 1784.

Page 10   "In the moment of our separation": GW to Lafayette, Dec. 8, 1784. *Writings,* vol. 28, p. 6.

"initiate two little children . . . and proper attention": GW to Tench Tilghman, June 2, 1785. *Writings,* vol. 28, p. 158.

"I am equally obliged to you, Sir": GW to Noah Webster, April 17, 1786. *Writings,* vol. 28, p. 409.

Page 10   "A little Grandson of Mrs. Washington's . . .": Tobias Lear to William Prescott, March 4, 1788. MVLA.

Page 11   "I began to repeat and love poetry": NC to EB, March 16, 1851. MVLA.

"I had no respect for my master . . . with deep regret": Eliza Custis to David Baille Warden, April 20, 1808. MVLA.

Page 12   "What should I have been if my blessed Grandmother": EB's draft of reminiscences, August 1852. MVLA.

Page 13   "Mrs. Washington has become too domestick": GW to Robert Morris, May 5, 1787. *Writings,* vol. 29, p. 210.

Page 14   "My movements to the chair of Government": GW to Henry Knox, April 1, 1789. *Writings,* vol. 30, p. 268.

"About 10 o'clock I bade adieu to Mount Vernon": GW diary entry, April 4, 1789. Washington, *Diaries of George Washington,* vol. 5, p. 445.

Page 15   "The children were a-bawling": Robert Morris, A Journey from Fredericksburg Virginia to New York, May 13-20, 1789.

"serious injury" "nervous fever": Eliza Custis to David Baille Warden, April 20, 1808. MVLA.

"Dear little Washington seemed to be lost in a maze": MW to Fanny Bassett Washington, June 8, 1789. MVLA.

Page 16   "spends her time at the window looking at carriages": Ibid.

"Reading, English . . . in London": Decatur, *Private Affairs of George Washington,* p. 86.

Page 18   "Mondays—Get some French by heart": NC, Manuscript French Exercise Book, January 4, 1792. MVLA.

Page 20   "shake hands with my Dear Boy . . . a mother": Eleanor Custis Stuart to Tobias Lear, August 19, 1789. MVLA.

"I am much alarm'd about my dear Nelly": Eleanor Custis Stuart to Tobias Lear, April 18, 1790. MVLA.

"a little wild creature": MW to Fanny Bassett, June 8, 1789. MVLA.

"I hope when Nelly has a little more gravatie": Martha Washington to Fanny Bassett, December 15, 1794. MVLA.

"You look as if your clothes . . . pains in dressing": NC to EB, January 29, 1833. MVLA.

"The form of Reception is this": Abigail Adams to Mary Cranch, August 9, 1789.

Page 21   "Mrs. Washington is a most friendly, good lady": Abigail Adams to Mary Cranch, July 12, 1789.

Page 22   "where the Sun always appears to shine": NC to EB, January 21, 1851. MVLA.

Page 23   "One evening my father's carriage was late in coming": Thane, *Mount Vernon Family,* p. 74.

"are fine girls. I think it is much to be lamented": Bourne, *First Family,* p. 135.

"gloomy mortal . . . heart broke": Eliza Custis to David Baille Warden, April 20, 1808. MVLA.

Page 24   "that destructive evil": NC to EB, June 23, 1815. MVLA.

Page 24   "At two lessons per week he engages to perfect any person": Sonneck, *Early Concert-Life in America*, p. 130.

Page 25   Nelly struck through the word "British" and wrote "American": "William & Ann," contained in bound volume of music, Volume II, Houghton Library, Harvard University.

Page 26   "He liked me to ask him for all that I wished to have": NC to EB, February 23, 1823. MVLA.

"As to the story of Nelly Custis, my sister": Custis, *Recollections and Private Memoirs of Washington*, p. 408.

"nor raise a note on any instrument": GW to Francis Hopkinson, February 5, 1789. *Writings*, vol. 30, p. 196.

"his presence chilled my young companions . . . which others did": NC to EB, February 23, 1823. MVLA.

Page 28   "an outrageous politician, perfectly *federal*": NC to EB, May 14, 1798. MVLA.

"We have a large company of the *Honorable Congress*": NC to EB, September 6, 1797. MVLA.

"livelier than ever": Susan Randolph to EB, n.d. [1794]. MVLA.

"Mr. Stuart goes on in the usual way": Bourne, *First Family*, p. 165.

Page 29   "was in no danger of being captivated by any one": NC to EB, October 19, 1795. MVLA.

"A hint here; men and women feel the same inclinations": Custis, *Recollections and Private Memoirs of Washington*, p. 42.

"Do not in your contemplation of the marriage state": GW to Eliza Custis, September 14, 1794. *Writings*, vol. 33, p. 500.

Page 30   "proper and necessary . . . to part from her": NC to EB, October 13, 1795. MVLA.

"I have gone through the greatest trial": NC to EB, October 19, 1795. MVLA.

"so many enchanting circumstances . . . submitting to the retired life": Eleanor Custis Stuart to Tobias Lear, June 8, 1789. MVLA.

Page 31   "Nelly is extremely homely in my opinion": NC to EB, March 30, 1796. MVLA.

"[I] wish you may have as much pleasure as you expect": MW to NC, 179[6?]. MVLA.

"I wish more & more every day": NC to EB, May 13, 1796. MVLA.

"A Missionary of Liberty to its Patriarch": Lafayette, *Letters of Lafayette to Washington*, p. 348.

Page 32   "I am as happy as a mortal can wish to be . . . the least inconvenience": NC to EB, September 6, 1796. MVLA.

"I can truly say I had rather be at home at Mount Vernon": GW to David Stuart, June 15, 1790. *Writings*, vol. 31, p. 49.

"terribly agitated": Moore, *The Family Life of George Washington*, p. 143.

"On one side I am called upon to remember": GW to Tobias Lear, March 9, 1797. *Writings*, vol. 37, p. 576.

Page 32   "no adventures of any kind . . . rowed us over in a barge": NC to EB, March 18, 1797. MVLA.

Page 33   "No consideration under heaven that I can foresee": GW to Robert Lewis, June 26, 1796. *Writings,* vol. 35, p. 99.

Page 34   "Since I left Philadelphia everything has appeared": NC to EB, March 18, 1797. MVLA.

"never found it too small, or too close . . . to a Palace away from her": NC to EB, October 10, 1832. MVLA.

Page 36   "I cannot tell you my dear friend, how much I enjoy home": Lossing, *Mary and Martha Washington,* p. 313.

"We are in a litter and dirt": GW to George Washington Parke Custis, April 3, 1797. *Writings,* vol. 35, p. 429.

"Grandpa is very well, & has already turned Farmer again": NC to EB, March 18, 1797. MVLA.

Page 37   "One day in retirement": NC to EB, February 23, 1823. MVLA.

Page 38   "every day to sing duetts . . . entirely to Solo's": NC to EB, July 2, 1797. MVLA.

"I have no objection to any sober or orderly persons": GW to William Pearce, November 23, 1794. *Writings,* vol. 34, p. 40.

"a well resorted tavern": GW to Mary Washington, February 15, 1787. *Writings,* vol. 29, p. 158.

"She appeared to be about twenty": Joshua Brooks, journal entry February 4, 1799. MVLA.

Page 39   "She was one of those celestial beings": Niemcewicz, *Under Their Vine and Fig Tree,* p. 97.

Page 40   "Miss Eleanor Custis . . . has more perfection of form": Latrobe, *The Journal of Latrobe,* pp. 57-58.

"I wish the world would not be so extremely busy": NC to EB, August 20, 1797. MVLA.

Page 41   "a little milk and water monkey": NC to EB, October 19, 1795. MVLA.

"too often told of his merits and accomplishments": NC to EB, May 30, 1797. MVLA.

"Young Mr. C. came here about a fortnight ago to dinner": GW to George Washington Parke Custis, April 15, 1798. *Writings,* vol. 36, p. 245.

"Mr Carroll was at Mount Vernon in March": NC to EB, May 14, 1798. MVLA.

"We can't get him to shoot himself": John Eager Howard to Benjamin Chew, Jr., February 22, 1814. Chew Family Papers, Historical Society of Pennsylvania.

Page 42   "From his infancy I have discovered": GW to Samuel Stanhope Smith, May 24, 1797. *Writings,* vol. 35, p. 450.

"He appears to me to be moped and stupid": GW to David Stuart, August 13, 1798. *Writings,* vol. 36, p. 412.

"so strikingly like her brother": Custis, *Recollections and Private Memoirs of Washington,* p. 147.

Page 43   "As both your aunt & I": GW to Lawrence Lewis, August 4, 1797. *Writings,* vol. 36, p. 2.

Page 43   "We expect Mr Lewis, a nephew of the President's": NC to EB, November 23, 1797. MVLA.

"I always have & do now, prefer the Country infinitely": NC to EB, March 20, 1798. MVLA.

Page 44   "We shall have black helmets, or morocco leather": NC to EB, May 14, 1798. MVLA.

"Grandpa, Mr Lewis and Mr Lear were taken sick": NC to EB, February 3, 1799. MVLA.

"without my having the smallest suspicion": GW to William Fitzhugh, January 25, 1799.

"was very curious about all my love letters": NC to EB, February 23, 1823. MVLA.

"Cupid, a small mischievous Urchin . . . calculated to ensure it": NC to EB, February 3, 1799. MVLA.

Page 45   "For me, my prospects of happiness although very great": Ibid.

"wither I went to become the guardian of Nelly": GW to Lawrence Lewis, January 23, 1799. *Writings,* vol. 37, p. 105.

"An event occurred on the twenty-second of February, 1799": Custis, *Recollections and Private Memoirs of Washington,* p. 450.

"something white . . . in a light flowered satin": Lee, *Growing Up in the 1850's,* p. 81.

Page 47   "Miss Custis was married": Washington, *Diaries,* vol.6, p. 335.

"I left my Beloved & revered GrandMama . . . attention in my power": NC to EB, November 4, 1799. MVLA.

"It has been understood from expressions": GW to Lawrence Lewis, September 20, 1799. *Writings,* vol. 37, p. 368.

Page 48   "The idea of being a Mother . . . a sedate matron": NC to EB, November 11, 1799. MVLA.

Page 49   Account of George Washington's final illness and death: Lear, *Letters & Recollections of George Washington,* pp. 129-135.

Page 50   "paying the last sad duties . . . The loss we have sustained is irreparable": NC to Mary Pinckney, January 12, 1800. MVLA.

"All is now over": Lear, *Letters & Recollections of George Washington,* p. 135.

"Frances is the darling of her good GrandMama . . . she takes a fancy to": NC to Mary Pinckney, May 1, 1801. MVLA.

Page 51   "one of the most detestable of mankind . . . his memory since his decease": William E. Curtis, Description of a Visit to "Lady" Washington, January 2, 1802. MVLA.

"You are misinformed": NC to EB, March 23, 1806. MVLA.

"My eldest sisters have been with us here since Christmas": NC to Mary Pinckney, January 3, 1802. MVLA.

Page 52   "Mrs. Washington appears much older . . . gave her particular pleasure": William E. Curtis, Description of a Visit to "Lady" Washington, January 2, 1802. MVLA.

"badly and had a wretched cold . . . no longer desirable": Cornelia Lee to Eliza Lee, March 14, 1802.

Page 52   "The pleasure which we had anticipated in this visit": Cope, *Philadelphia Merchant: The Diary of Thomas P. Cope, 1800-1851*, pp. 111-112.

Page 53   "the honors of the House and Table . . . called to action": Portia Lee Hodgson, June 1, 1802.

The Woodlawn Years

Page 56   "well and comfortably fixed": NC to Mary Pinckney, May 9, 1801. MVLA.

Page 57   "that neither time or the variety of changes": NC to EB, December 4, 1804. MVLA.

"sickness and sorrow": NC to EB, March 23, 1806. MVLA.

"Ah my Beloved friend, how sadly times are changed to us all": NC to EB, March 23, 1806. MVLA.

"Her tenderness and unceasing care of me": NC to EB, January 11, 1805. MVLA.

Page 59   "I live now in sight of Mount Vernon": Moore, *The Family Life of George Washington*, p. 170.

"Their house, after the manner of that part of the country": Judge David Daggett to Susan Daggett, December 26, 1817.

"It is not a Virginia fashion to pay *short* visits": NC to EB, July 4, 1817. MVLA.

Page 60   "an elegant parlour, well stocked": "Two Early Visitors to Mount Vernon" from Journal of "A Scot Recently Come Over," *New-York Historical Society Quarterly*, XLII (October 1958), p. 364.

"his chest will not bear the flute . . . plays a tune decently": NC to EB, November 10, 1822. MVLA.

Page 61   "give up music & painting": NC to EB, July 4, 1817. MVLA.

Page 62   "1 pint of dough": Lewis, *Housekeeping Book*, p. 79.

"The table was spread with double cloths": Thomas Hill Hubbard, "Political and Social Life in Washington during the Administration of James Monroe," *Oneida Historical Society Bulletin*, 1903, p. 70.

Page 63   "before one was out of his room": NC to EB, June 25, 1823. MVLA.

"I could not live without them": Ibid.

Page 65   "I hope you will pardon the trouble I give you": NC to EB, March 19, 1822. MVLA.

"They are all too large": NC to EB, December 3, 1821. MVLA.

"Father wishes to have a wig": Frances Parke Custis Lewis to EB, November 1820. MVLA.

"into the inside of the stage": NC to EB, January 1 1824. MVLA.

Page 67   "Her motto, 'Amour Maternelle'": EB's draft of reminiscences, August 1852. MVLA.

"released from a sorrowful world": NC to EB, January 11, 1805. MVLA.

Page 68   "Life has no charm for me": Ibid.

Page 70　"no delight equal to nursing": NC to Mary Pinckney, April 24, 1800. MVLA.

"endeavour'd to reconcile them for their childs sake": NC to EB, August 25, 1811. MVLA.

Page 71　"I believe I am not well calculated for an instructress": NC to EB, March 23, 1806. MVLA.

"an excellent talent for drawing . . . becoming a humdrum character": NC to EB, August 25, 1811. MVLA.

"It was indeed a severe trial": NC to EB, January 3, 1815. MVLA.

Page 72　"Excuse the anxiety of a Mother . . . from your protecting care": Ibid.

Page 73　"happiness to much, to deprive her": NC to EB, July 23, 1815. MVLA.

"Mr Lewis was seized with the gout . . . to suppose in danger": Ibid.

"remind her, whenever she is with you": NC to EB, late July 1815. MVLA.

Page 74　"I cannot give up nursing her myself": NC to EB, October 1820. MVLA.

"Your Angel sister went off": NC to Frances Parke Lewis, October 1820. MVLA.

"They say my Child has not changed yet": NC to EB, October 30, 1820. MVLA.

"be put into the Vault in less than three days after I am dead": Lear, *Letters & Recollections of George Washington,* p. 134.

"She is ever before me": NC to EB, November 20, 1820. MVLA.

"I regret most bitterly": NC to EB, November 22, 1820. MVLA.

Page 75　"To the spot thou most loved do I repair": NC to EB, January 3, 1822. MVLA.

"We had a long conversation at night": NC to EB, January 25, 1821. MVLA.

Page 76　"In less than thirty months": NC to EB, October 14, 1822. MVLA.

"the misfortune of living on a Virga Farm": NC to EB, April 23, 1821. MVLA.

"from the idle life . . . will be of lasting advantage": NC to EB, May 7, 1823. MVLA.

"I am doing all in my power for her myself": NC to EB, October 7, 1825. MVLA.

Page 77　"She sleeps in my bosom always": NC to EB, October 2, 1825. MVLA.

"Oh for a house in Chestnut Street": NC to EB, November 10, 1822. MVLA.

"I am almost a vegetable": NC to EB, January 15, 1823. MVLA.

Page 78　"one who almost idolized the Gen'l and Grandmama": NC to EB, August 10, 1824. MVLA.

Page 79　"I went to a drawing room": NC to EB, March 4, 1822. MVLA.

"The papers will tell you of our disappointments": NC to EB, February 15, 1825. MVLA.

"Poor George is most painfully situated": Ibid.

Page 80   "I am happy to think that you have received from my Father": NC to EB, October 2, 1825. MVLA.

"we have had the happiness to receive him here": EB to NC, December 22, 1824. MVLA.

"It appears now like a pleasant dream": NC to EB, October 7, 1825. MVLA.

"I am in raptures with it": NC to EB, June 21, 1826. MVLA.

"There is a perfect rage for marrying this year": NC to EB, December 2, 1823. MVLA.

Page 81   "I know too well": NC to EB, November 24, 1820. MVLA.

Nelly's support of gradual emancipation: NC to EB, March 19, 1832. MVLA.

"May she continue free from the spell": EB to NC, January 21, 1821. MVLA.

"what real greatness consists in": NC to EB, January 11, 1821. MVLA.

"indifferent to all sons of Adam": NC to EB, November 15, 1823. MVLA.

Page 82   Nelly's efforts to thwart an inadequate suitor: NC to EB, December 3, 1821. MVLA.

"He has been much in the world": NC to EB, January 14, 1824. MVLA.

"He is the choice of my dear Child": NC to EB, April 5, 1825. MVLA.

Page 84   "*smiled* his determination to redeem the Pledge": NC to EB, December 24, 1826. MVLA.

"My poor Parke": July 6, 1829. MVLA.

"I rejoice that I can without hesitation": NC to EB, February 12, 1826. MVLA.

Page 85   "we always share the same bed": NC to EB, October 10, 1832. MVLA.

"I trust you will not permit": NC to EB, January 29, 1833. MVLA.

Page 86   "Sunday among the French & Creoles": Ibid.

"literally buried alive, her health her spirits destroy'd": NC to EB, July 27, 1836. MVLA.

"Indeed he is all I have ever known or heard of": NC to EB, June 20, 1835. MVLA.

Page 87   "Mr L intends to buy a small place": NC to EB, March 23, 1835. MVLA.

"Of eight children I have outlived six": NC to EB, November 5, 1839. MVLA.

Page 88   "Woodlawn is worse than nothing": Lawrence Lewis to Edward George Washington Butler, January 18, 1837. MVLA.

Page 89   "Our Farm here never very productive is worse than ever": NC to EB, March 23, 1835. MVLA.

"the subject to her mother": Lawrence Lewis to Edward George Washington Butler, January 18, 1837. MVLA.

Page 90   "Her husband, Major Lawrence Lewis": EB's draft of reminiscences, August 1852. MVLA.

"Mr L is not the most energetic of men": NC to EB, March 1, 1815. MVLA.

Page 91   "I owe him a *grudge*": NC to EB, July 21, 1821. MVLA.

"exiled": NC to EB, January 17, 1826. MVLA.

"I often wish that I could go back again": NC to EB, December 9, 1843. MVLA.

"an old relick of past happy times": NC to EB, March 22, 1887. MVLA.

Page 92   "I was only six years old at that time": NC to George Washington Parke Custis, December 3, 1849. MVLA.

Page 93   "I crept into your heart slyly": NC to EB, March 1, 1815. MVLA.

"he moved to La. to get as far from me as possible": NC to EB, December 20, 1840. MVLA.

Page 94   "ten years of sorrow & privations": Ibid.

"after so many years without religious service": NC to EB, December 10, 1844. MVLA.

Page 95   "I candidly confess": NC to EB, October 23, 1851. MVLA.

Audley: The Last Years

Page 98   "If you had our *seven* boys in your house": NC to EB, December 10, 1844. MVLA.

Page 99   "chok full of fight but received no call": NC to EB, April 20, 1848. MVLA.

"You will be sorry to hear that Robt Lee": NC to EB, August 29, 1846. MVLA.

"& he will walk in *his* steps": NC to EB, December 17, 1848. MVLA.

Page 100   "Poor Mrs. Taylor is seldom quite well": NC to Markie Williams, March 25, 1849. MVLA.

"to go at no distant day": NC to EB, December 1, 1850. MVLA.

"I felt convinced that I ought to feel *grateful*": NC to EB, July 27, 1850. MVLA.

"All the trees, the hedge, the flower knot": NC to EB, 1851. MVLA.

Page 101   "This beautiful autumn I cannot participate in": NC to EB, December 1, 1850. MVLA.

"I recall him to my mind *now*": NC to EB, January 21, 1851. MVLA.

Page 102   "Did I not with *my whole heart*": NC to EB, Ibid.

BIBLIOGRAPHY

Beldon, Louise Conway. *The Festive Tradition: Table Decorations and Desserts in America, 1650-1900*. New York: W.W. Norton & Company, 1983.

Bourne, Miriam Anne. *First Family: George Washington and his Intimate Relations*. New York: W.W. Norton & Company, 1982.

Britt, Judith S. *Nothing More Agreeable: Music in George Washington's Family*. Mount Vernon: Mount Vernon Ladies' Association, 1984.

Carroll, John Alexander, and Ashworth, Mary Wells. *George Washington, Vol. 7: First in Peace*. New York: Charles Scribner's Sons, 1957.

Cope, Thomas P. *Philadelphia Merchant: The Diary of Thomas P. Cope, 1800-1851*. South Bend: Gateway Editions, 1978.

Custis, George Washington Parke. *Recollections and Private Memoirs of Washington*. New York: Derby & Jackson, 1860.

De Pauw, Linda Grant. *Founding Mothers: Women of America in the Revolutionary Era*. Boston: Houghton Mifflin Company, 1975.

Decatur, Stephen, Jr. *Private Affairs of George Washington, From the Records and Accounts of Tobias Lear, Esquire, his Secretary*. Boston: Houghton Mifflin Company, 1933.

Detweiler, Susan Gray. *George Washington's Chinaware*. New York: Harry N. Abrams, Inc., 1982.

Duke, Jane Taylor. *Kenmore and the Lewises*. Fredericksburg: Kenmore Association, Incorporated, 1965.

Ferling, John E. *The First of Men: A Life of George Washington*. Knoxville: University of Tennessee Press, 1988.

Freeman, Douglas Southall. *George Washington: A Biography*. 6 vols. New York: Charles Scribner's Sons, 1942-52.

Hess, Karen. *Martha Washington's Booke of Cookery*. New York: Columbia University Press, 1981.

Idzerda, Stanley J., Loveland, Anne C., and Miller, Marc H. *Lafayette, Hero of Two Worlds*. Hanover: University Press of New England, 1989.

Lafayette, Marquis de. *Letters of Lafayette to Washington, 1777-1799*. Edited by Louis Gottschalk. New York: Helen F. Hubbard, 1944.

Larkin, Jack. *The Reshaping of Everyday Life, 1790-1840*. New York: Harper & Row, 1988.

Latrobe, Benjamin Henry. *The Journal of Latrobe*. New York: D. Appleton and Company, 1905.

Lear, Tobias. *Letters & Recollections of George Washington*. Garden City: Doubleday, Doran & Company, Inc., 1932.

Lee, Agnes. *Growing Up in the 1850's: The Journal of Agnes Lee*. Edited by Mary Custis Lee DeButts. Chapel Hill: University of North Carolina Press, 1984.

Lewis, Jan. *The Pursuit of Happiness: Family and Values in Jefferson's Virginia.* Cambridge: Cambridge University Press, 1983.

Lewis, Nelly Custis. *Housekeeping Book.* Edited by Patricia Brady Schmit. New Orleans: Historic New Orleans Collection, 1982.

Lossing, Benson. *Mary and Martha.* New York: Harper & Brothers, 1886.

Lowther, Minnie Kendall. *Mount Vernon: Its Children, Its Romances, Its Allied Families and Mansions.* Chicago: John C. Winston Company, 1932.

Moore, Charles. *The Family Life of George Washington.* Boston: Houghton Mifflin Company, 1926.

Niemcewicz, Julian Ursyn. *Under Their Vine and Fig Tree: Travels Through America in 1797-1799.* Translated and edited by Metchie J.E. Budka. Elizabeth, NJ: Grassmann Publishing Company, 1965.

Norton, Mary Beth. *Liberty's Daughters: The Revolutionary Experience of American Woman, 1750-1800.* Boston: Little, Brown and Company, 1980.

Powell, J. H. *Bring Out Your Dead: The Great Plague of Yellow Fever in Philadelphia in 1793.* Philadelphia: University of Pennsylvania Press, 1949.

Slaughter, Thomas P. *The Whiskey Rebellion: Frontier Epilogue to the American Revolution.* New York: Oxford University Press, 1986.

Sonneck, O.G. *Early Concert-Life in America (1731-1800).* Leipzig: Breitkopf & Hartel, 1969.

Spruill, Julia Cherry. *Women's Life & Work in the Southern Colonies.* New York: W.W. Norton & Company, 1972.

Thane, Elswyth. *Mount Vernon Family.* New York: Macmillan Company, 1968.

_____. *Mount Vernon Is Ours.* New York: Duell, Sloan and Pearce, 1966.

_____. *Mount Vernon: The Legacy.* Philadelphia: J.B. Lippincott Company, 1967.

_____. *Potomac Squire.* Mount Vernon: Mount Vernon Ladies' Association, 1963.

Torbert, Alice Coyle. *Eleanor Calvert and Her Circle.* New York: William-Frederick Press, 1950.

Wall, Charles Cecil. *George Washington: Citizen-Soldier.* Mount Vernon: Mount Vernon Ladies' Association, 1988.

Washington, George. *The Diaries of George Washington.* Edited by Donald Jackson and Dorothy Twohig. 6 vols. Charlotesville: University Press of Virginia, 1976-79.

_____. *The Writings of George Washington.* Edited by John C. Fitzpatrick. 39 vols. Washington D.C.: U.S. Government Printing Office, 1931-44.

Wayland, John W. *The Washingtons and Their Homes.* Berryville: Virginia Book Company, 1944.

Withey, Lynne. *Dearest Friend: A Life of Abigail Adams.* New York: Macmillan Publishing Co., Inc., 1981.

INDEX

Adams, Abigail, 21
Adams, John, 32, 43-44, 56, 79
Adams, John Quincy, 79
Abingdon, 2, 5, 15
Allen, Andrew, 101
Arlington, 60, 77, 93
Audley, 84, 87, 95, 98

Bassett, Burwell, 3
Bordley, Elizabeth. *See* Gibson,
  Elizabeth Bordley.
Bordley, John Beale, 22
Brooks, Joshua, 38
Butler, Edward, Jr., 98
Butler, Edward George Washington,
  82-84, 85-86, 93-95
Butler, Frances Parke Lewis, 48, 50-51,
  52, 60, 85-86
  birth, 48
  education, 71-73
  in Philadelphia, 71-73
  marriage to Edward George
    Washington Butler, 83
  in Louisiana, 85-86, 94

Capron, Henry, 24
Carroll, Charles, 41
Carter, Betty, 57
Conrad, Charles Magill, 86, 98
Conrad, Mary Eliza Angela Lewis,
  68, 86
  death, 87
  education, 76-77, 80
  in Philadelphia, 85
  marriage to Charles Magill Conrad,
    86
Cope, Thomas P., 52
Coxe, John Redmond, 84
Craik, James, 3, 50, 52
Cunningham, Ann Pamela, 100
Curtis, William E., 52
Custis, Daniel Parke, 5
Custis, Eleanor Calvert, 2, 3, 4-8, 28
  attitude toward children, 6-8, 20, 70
  death, 67

Custis, Eleanor Parke ("Nelly"). *See*
  Lewis, Eleanor Parke Custis
Custis, Eliza Parke. *See* Law, Eliza
  Parke Custis
Custis, George Washington Parke, 92
  education, 41-42
  youth, 14-15
Custis, John Parke ("Jacky"), 2, 48
  education, 5
  enlistment in Continental Army, 3
  death, 3
Custis, Martha Parke ("Patsy"), 5
Custis, Martha Parke ("Patty"). *See*
  Peter, Martha Parke Custis

Daggett, David, 59
Dandridge, Bartholomew, 3-4, 5, 44
Davis, Reverend Thomas, 45, 50
Dunboyne Plantation, 85-86, 93
Dunlap, William, 18

Eltham, 3

Fay, Reverend and Mrs., 94
Fenno, John, 19
Fraunces' Tavern, 4

Gaines, Edmund Pendleton, 83, 85
Gibson, Elizabeth Bordley, 22-23, 38,
  57, 64-66, 71, 72-75, 76-77, 79, 81,
  85, 90, 93, 98, 101-102
Gibson, James, 73, 76
Graham, Isabella, 16-18
Gray's Hill. *See* Woodlawn
Greland, Madame, 71, 73, 74-75

Hamilton, Alexander, 27
harpsichord, 26, 37-38, 59, 95, 100
Hope Park, 23, 28, 30-31
Houdon, Jean Antoine, 92
Hubbard, Thomas Hill, 62-63
Humphreys, David, 11, 14

Isaac House, 24